Tex
Photography: Chris Bradley
Managing Editor: Clare Peel
Series Editor: Tony Halliday

Berlitz POCKET GUIDE

Libya

First Edition 2006

PHOTOGRAPHY
Chris Bradley/Apa
Cover photograph: Chris Bradley/Apa

CONTACTING THE EDITORS
Every effort has been made to provide accurate information in this publication, but changes are inevitable. The publisher cannot be responsible for any resulting loss, inconvenience or injury. We would appreciate it if readers would call our attention to any errors or outdated information by contacting Berlitz Publishing, PO Box 7910, London SE1 1WE, England. Fax: (44) 20 7403 0290.
email: berlitz@apaguide.co.uk
www.berlitzpublishing.com

The coastal ruins and magnificent Roman Theatre of Sabratha (page 50)

War graves at Tobruk (page 82) are a sobering reminder of the North African campaign

Leptis Magna (page 39) is the best-preserved ancient Roman city in the world

TOP TEN ATTRACTIONS

The Medina in Tripoli (page 30) is a maze of alleyways, mosques and restored mansions

The Ubari Lakes (page 86) are amazing natural wonders in an expanse of giant sand dunes

The Old City of Ghadames (page 62) is a magical ghost town in the desert

The fortified granaries of Jebel Nafusa (page 57) are typical of Berber ingenuity

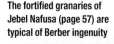

Astounding rock art (page 88) makes the Fezzan region one giant open-air museum

The ancient port of Ptolemais (page 69) was once a very wealthy city

Cyrene (page 73) was the most important Greek city in Africa

CONTENTS

INTRODUCTION

L ibya's international re-emergence has created an exciting new Mediterranean destination of world-class sites. Its history is a unique mixture of ancient Greek, Roman, Byzantine, Arab and Ottoman rule, underpinned by Islam from the 7th century. Add to this a veneer of Italian colonialism and a fluctuating history since independence and you have a destination unlike any other. As tourism opens the door into this hidden world, visitors can experience an exotic blend of Africa and the Middle East and Mediterranean.

Libya has a vast and varied landscape, from the lush forests of the Green Mountains to the endless Saharan sands. The desert regions make up over 90 percent of the country and are spectacularly rugged, with monumental eroded mountains and remarkable natural lakes. The Mediterranean coastline runs along the north, while the longest border is in the east with Egypt. Tunisia and Algeria lie to the west, and in the south are the remote desert frontiers with Sudan, Niger and Chad, where the Tibesti Mountains reach Libya's highest point. For thousands of years Libya has been the link between Africa and Europe, and the region has been greatly influenced by both. It also links the Magreb with the rest of the Arab world.

> Seven times the size of the UK, Libya is the fourth-largest country in Africa, with an area of 1,760,000 sq km (680,000 sq miles).

More than 85 percent of the 5.6 million population live along the fertile and well-watered Mediterranean coast, where all the major cities are situated. Agriculture employs the greatest number of people, and produces wheat, barley,

Inside the Old City of Ghadames, the 'Pearl of the Desert'

Touareg with loaded tourist camels in the Acacus Mountains

olives, citrus, dates, vegetables, nuts, soya beans and cattle. Majestic date palms and rugged olive trees have traditionally been cherished in Libya.

With a lack of natural barriers, the climate is influenced by the Mediterranean in the north and the Sahara in the south. Coastal regions have a pleasant Mediterranean climate with moderate temperatures and sufficient rain for widespread agriculture. In winter it can get very wet and cold in Cyrenaica, thanks to the altitude. In the desert, temperatures can rise to 58°C (136°F) and droughts are frequent, but even a short downpour quickly turns the desert into a carpet of new flowers. Away from the main population centres, the desert is the perfect environment for camels, snakes and even limited numbers of fennec foxes, gazelles and jackals.

The mystical natural oases of the Ubari Sand Sea provide sustenance for date palms, fig trees and even humans, who somehow survive by eating and trading a mash made from the tiny red shrimps in the lakes. Wherever you travel there is always the accompanying sound of birdsong, even in the Sahara, where the oases are used by birds migrating to and from Africa.

Ancient Culture

Tripolitania in the west is the area of the three ancient cities of Leptis Magna, Sabratha and Oea (modern Tripoli), and still has the highest concentration of population in Libya, with large towns every few kilometres. These sites of antiquity are considered some of the most important and best-preserved Roman cities in the world.

The Jebel Nafusa mountains rising up behind the 50-km (30-mile) wide Jefara Plain have for millennia been used as a place of refuge by the indigenous Berber tribes, escaping every invader coming along the coast. The desert people of Ghadames use every part of the precious palm trees of the oases to build their unique city of covered streets to protect themselves from the burning sun. In the far south, it is only the Touareg people who can survive in the middle of the Sahara, guiding tourist groups today, just as they have always controlled desert trade.

Water that is trapped deep below ground is now being pumped to the heavily populated coast in a tremendous feat of engineering. The Great Man-Made River Project is slowly unlocking the water from underground desert reservoirs and piping it thousands of kilometres further north, where it is most needed. It is one of the

Marble relief, Sabratha

largest civil-engineering projects in the world today. Started in 1984, it currently consists of 5,000km (3,000 miles) of underground pipes connecting the stores of fresh water deep under the Sahara with the populated but poorly watered northern coast. The water has been undisturbed for at least 15,000 years, and its total amount is estimated to equal the discharge of the River Nile for over 200 years.

Cyrenaica in the northeast is an area rich in Greek archaeological ruins, where the people have more in common with their Egyptian neighbours than with their countrymen from Tripolitania. The land of the Jebel al-Akhdar (Green Mountains) is more rugged and receives ample rainfall, as anyone caught in a freezing downpour in winter can testify. Hardy shepherds and their flocks wander among a great variety of mountain crops, past ancient Greek ruins and old Italian colonial farmhouses.

Great Man-Made River Project under construction at Ras Lanuf

Libyan Society

Since independence, there has been a reaffirmation of Islamic values, and modern Libyans adhere to the traditions of a Muslim society revolving around family life. A typical family might include a man and wife, unmarried children, married sons with their families, elderly parents, plus any unmarried sisters and aunts. As elsewhere, many young couples try to set up their own homes, rather than living with the

Touareg man, Fezzan region

husband's parents. Some marriages are arranged by parents, but today many young urbanites choose their own partners. Wedding celebrations may still last a week in rural areas but are often limited by expense to a few days in the cities.

In Libya, men are the main wage-earners and are regarded as the head of the family, while women are responsible for maintaining the home. Previously, few women went to school, and outside of the house were veiled and had a family escort. Many younger women in the cities are now continuing their free education on to college and university, with careers in teaching and nursing. For subjects including medicine, agriculture and engineering, university students can study abroad on state-paid grants, but few of these are women.

The overall impression is of a relatively stable society whose people are neither very rich nor particularly poor. There is none of the ostentatious wealth of the Gulf States, but equally no begging in the streets. Oil revenues combined with a small population give Libya one of the highest

The Roman Theatre at Sabratha

per capita GDPs in Africa, but little of this income flows down to the lower levels of society, many of whom are immigrants from sub-Saharan countries seeking a better life.

Tourism and Libya

For the historians there are the magnificent cities of Leptis Magna, Sabratha, Cyrene and countless other sites. Culture-lovers will revel in the dramatic Berber strongholds of Jebel Nafusa and the medinas of Tripoli or Ghadames, while adventurers have a million square kilometres in which to enjoy the wilds of the Sahara and glimpse its ancient way of life through pre-historic rock paintings.

Most Libyans are friendly and genuinely interested in where you come from, knowing that you will have overcome certain reservations just to be here. To avoid causing offence it is better to dress conservatively, with trousers and long-sleeved shirts for both sexes; this also serves as sensible protection from the sun. Women should avoid wearing short skirts and tight tops, and must cover their heads when visiting any religious sites.

At present tourists face little hassle in *souqs* or shops, compared to other North African countries, but as tourism increases this is bound to change. Even tipping is something that Libyans in the tourism industry are just getting used to. The newly formed Ministry of Tourism plans to create 'tourism resorts' along the coast – so get to Libya before it changes too much into a truly international destination.

A BRIEF HISTORY

Local Berber tribes of western Libya probably developed around 10,000 years ago from nomadic hunters of Western Asia, who established themselves in the mountain regions stretching to the Atlantic coast. At about the same time there is the evidence of the earliest rock art, proving there was human activity deep in the Sahara, when the climate was more moderate.

Phoenician trading depots were established along the North African coast before 1000BC, carrying minerals from the Iberian peninsula to the Levant, with overland trade from deep in the Sahara. These desert routes from the Niger and Nile rivers were controlled by the mysterious Garamantians, who established a powerful kingdom around their capital Germa.

Rock carvings from the M'sak Settafet region in Germa Museum

Greek traders who encountered the local Berbers called them *barbaroi*, meaning 'not speaking Greek' or 'uncivilised'. This, in turn, gave rise to the two words Berber and barbarian.

Phoenician Traders

Over 3,000 years ago it was the Greeks who were the sea-faring masters of the Mediterranean, with ports all along the European coastline. But their supremacy was challenged by Phoenician traders based at Tyre and Sidon (in present-day Lebanon) who developed an alternative sea route along the North African coast to the valuable ore mines of the Iberian peninsula. Because of their good mooring facilities, three coastal settlements were established, at Oea (now Tripoli), Labda (Leptis Magna) and Sabratha, in a region often referred to as Tripolitania – the 'Three Cities'.

After Tyre and Sidon fell to the Persians in the 6th century BC, Carthage (further west, in modern Tunisia) became the dominant city of this trade, developing its own autonomy and Punic (Phoenician-style) civilisation. The indigenous Berbers in their mountain strongholds worked alongside them, and assimilated Punic cults, practices and language, some of which still remain to this day.

By the 3rd century BC Roman expansion brought the two powers into conflict, resulting in the three Punic wars (264–146BC) and the eventual destruction of Carthage. The victorious Romans placed Tripolitania in the hands of their Berber allies from Numidia (modern Algeria) until a century later, when Julius Ceasar reclaimed the territory and annexed it as a Roman province.

> **The name 'Libya' is an ancient word used by the Romans to describe this region, and probably derives from the 'Libue' people mentioned by Herodotus as living south of the Mediterranean.**

The Greeks in Cyrenaica

The coastline of North Africa is only 300km (185 miles) from Crete, and thus had long been within the sphere of Greek influence. Hellenic expansion in the 7th century BC brought new colonies into Cyrenaica, particularly from the island of Thira (Santorini), whose inhabitants were told by the oracle at Delphi to find a new fertile home in Africa. Thus in 631BC they founded the city of Cyrene (hence the name Cyrenaica), away from the coast in fertile highlands with ample rainfall.

In 525BC Cambyses, the son of Persian King Cyrus the Great, swept in from Egypt, and Cyrenaica came under Egyptian (or Persian) rule for almost two centuries. Alexander the Great retook the area for Greece in 331BC during his Egyptian campaigns, but his death and the subdivision of his empire to his generals led to a period of uncertainty, and also the establishing of the important Pentapolis ('Five Cities'). Further expansion was only halted by the annexation of the area by the Romans in 74BC.

Mosaic of Medusa, Ptolemais

The Romans

By controlling eastern and western Libya during the 1st century BC, the Romans brought a system of government and common language to the inhabitants – mainly Berber farmers. In return they inherited a fertile region that would become the food store of the Roman Empire. Grain and olive oil flowed from the developing urban centres of Leptis Magna and Sabratha, while Cyrenaica provided wine and domestic animals. Further south, the Garamantians acted as desert overseers, supplying gold, slaves and animals from beyond the Sahara.

The only obstacles to complete Roman domination were the fiercely independent Berber tribes of the central desert region around Sirte, who severely hampered communication and trade between Tripolitania and Cyrenaica. It was only towards the end of the 1st century AD that all threats were quashed and there was safe movement of people and goods along a series of coastal Roman roads, secured by local legions and garrisons, and treaties with local tribes.

Sabratha's Roman remains

The city of Cyrene was severely damaged in AD115 by a Jewish uprising, and further destroyed – like most of Libya's other major sites – in the great earthquake of AD365. The split between east and west was magnified even more with the collapse of the old Roman order after 395, at which time Tripolitania aligned with Rome, while Cyrenaica came under control of the Coptic Patriarch in Alexandria. Each church developed its own identity, but it was generally a time of political, economic and religious unrest.

Into this turmoil in the first half of the 5th century came the Germanic tribe of the Vandals, who plundered the riches of Tripolitania while still allowing nominal control from Rome. But the Vandals were a spent force by 533, when the Byzantine general Belisarius reconquered the western Libyan coast and nominally reunited the country. Although it

The Libyan Septimius Severus became Emperor of Rome in 197

prevailed for over a century, Byzantine control was generally characterised by high taxes, insecurity, decaying public services and the rising power of inland Berber tribes.

The Arab Conquest

Following the death of the Prophet Mohammed in 632, a wave of Islamic expansion spread out of Arabia and along the North African coast. By 642 Cyrenaica was under the control of the army of the Caliph (the successor to the Prophet), but westward expansion slowed as the Arab armies faced strong Berber resistance to yet another invader.

The Muslim conquerers did not seek to colonise, but to assimilate themselves into the remains of Berber society, bringing social and religious conformity to a region suffering from Byzantine decay. Many Berbers (and Christians) welcomed the security that the 'Islamic missionaries' brought, allowing trade to flourish once again, while others resented them as tax-collecting soldiers. The Byzantine forts in Tripolitania were taken, but it was almost another 20 years before Arab general Uqba bin Nafi finally controlled the Fezzan in 663.

Over the next 30 years many Berber tribes initially resisted but then embraced Islam, eventually allowing Uqba to take the important Byzantine stronghold of Carthage and establish the holy city of Kairouan. By 710 the entire Magreb had fallen under Islamic control, and it was from here that the Arabs invaded Andalusia within five years.

The Berbers then set about altering Islam to their liking by encompassing local practices, which also had the advantage of distinguishing them from the Arabs, now controlled from Damascus. One of the local sects that flourished throughout the 8th century was the Kharijites (the name means 'those who emerge from impropriety'). Their minor tribal kingdom flourished as the Arabs struggled to maintain control, when the Umayyid Caliphate was being wrestled from Damascus by the Abbassids in Baghdad.

A fortified Berber granary in Kabaw, western Nafusa

One of the most important developments at this time in the Fezzan was the success of the Beni Khattab tribe in founding their own kingdom at Zuwaylah, which became an important trans-Saharan trade centre.

In 800 the Abbassid Caliph Harun ar-Rashid allowed Amir Ibrahim ibn-Aghlab autonomy to redevelop the neglected Roman infrastructure, such as the irrigation systems. Agriculture, trade and prosperity followed for the area under the control of Kairouan, which included Tripolitania. For over a century his successors, known as the Aghlabid Amirs, welcomed respected scholars, officials and merchants from around the Islamic world, as well as Jews and Christians, to establish an urban elite who went on to seize Sicily and much of Italy, and ultimately to challenge Byzantium.

The split between the Shia and Sunni branches of Islam led to fighting for control, which ended when the Fatimids (the Shia group named after the Prophet's daughter Fatima) rose up and created their new capital in Cairo. In the 11th century discontented Berbers threatened to return Libya to Sunni orthodoxy, a threat that was countered by the Fatimids inviting Bedouin tribes known as the Hilalians (Beni Hilal and Beni Salim tribes) to crush the rebellion. In doing so they wrecked most of the infrastructure, and it was into this void that the Norman rulers attacked from Sicily in the 12th century. They managed to control coastal trade but little else.

When the Almohads of Morocco were replaced by the Hafsids based in Tunis, there began a 350-year domination of Tripolitania – a state that encouraged trade, learning and the arts.

Arrival of the Ottomans

Cyrenaica was nominally under the control of Mamluk Egyptian rulers, an uneasy state of affairs which lasted until the 16th century, when Ottoman Turks came to challenge Spanish control of the central Mediterranean. The defence of Tripoli was in the hands of the Knights of St John of Malta, as renegade pirates such as Barbarossa played one side against the other. The control of trade became a free for all, until the Turkish admiral Sinan Pasha ousted the Knights and Libya settled into 360 years of Ottoman control that did not end until 1911.

The Ottomans divided their new territories into three regencies based on Algiers, Tunis and Tripoli, and set about controlling them with military Janissaries, who mutinied from time to time to gain control for themselves. In 1711 Ahmed Karamanli seized power and began a family dynasty that would last more than a century, during which many mosques and fine houses that can still be seen today were built in Tripoli's Medina. The wealth of the Karamanlis came initially from the control of piracy and then from payments made by European and US merchant ships that the Karamanlis protected.

But the rise of European naval power in the 19th century put an end to corsair attacks, and when Ali Karamanli asked for Ottoman help in 1835 to repel increased European aggression, the Turks swept him aside, and Sultan Mohammed II retook control direct from Constantinople. By this time Cyrenaica had become a separate province, increasingly under the spiritual control of Mohammed bin Ali as-Sanusi, a Sufi holy man from Algeria. He established the Sanusi order in al-Jaghbub, south of Tobruk on the desert Haj pilgrim route. Many of the attributes of Sanusi lifestyle were attractive to the Bedouin tribesmen, and it became a loose organisation that represented opposition to Ottoman and increasingly European influence along the coast.

Italian colonisation even stretched to their love of motor racing when a new Grand Prix circuit was added to the calendar – the Autodromo di Mellaha. At the time it was the fastest road-racing circuit in the world, and hosted the Tripoli Grand Prix throughout the 1930s.

Remains of the Philaeni Brothers Arch, near Sirte

Italian Colonists

The Italians were latecomers in the European scramble for colonies, and took their opportunity by manipulating a confrontation with a weakened Ottoman Empire in 1911. The Turks withdrew and Italy set about colonising the fertile coastal farmland. But Sanusi followers in Cyrenaica were hostile to the infidels replacing Muslim control, and the First Italian–Sanusi War (1914–17) became an intriguing struggle within World War I.

After the war, Italy under Mussolini proceeded with its colonisation at great pace throughout Tripolitania, which could offer no coherent opposition (unlike the Sanusis in Cyrenaica, now led by Idris). The Second Italian–Sanusi War (1923–31) saw the emergence of charismatic freedom fighters such as Omar al-Mukhtar, the 'Lion of the Desert', who was captured and publicly hanged in Benghazi in 1931. A period of stability saw Tripoli develop grandly, with

imposing buildings and new thoroughfares. This new peace
allowed Italy to organise fully the settling of Italian families
on allocated farmland, and by 1940 there were an estimated
110,000 settlers.

War in the Desert

World War II brought all this to an end, as the coastal strip
witnessed the ebb and flow of warfare between the Allied and
Axis powers. Between 1940 and 1943 huge columns of tanks
and men fought for control, with Montgomery and Rommel
striving to outwit each other strategically. Defeat for Germany and Italy placed Britain as the occupying force in
Tripolitania and Cyrenaica, while France controlled
Ghadames, Ghat and the rest of the Fezzan. As leader of the
Sanusi, Idris was the logical national leader, even though he
really represented only Cyrenaican interests. It was to him
that the UN granted independence on 24 December 1951.

King Idris was a hesitant leader of a poor country, who relied on the presence of British and American air bases for
stability. The discovery of oil in 1959 gave a boost to the
economy, but the future was uncertain, as the ageing Idris
had no son or obvious successor, and anti-Western demonstrations increased, inspired by Nasser's revolution in Egypt.

The September 1969 Coup

A large number of army officers waited until King Idris was
out of the country before launching their coup d'état in
Benghazi. Inside two hours they had taken control of the
government and abolished the monarchy. The coup, backed
by the army, was generally popular, especially among the
young. A free and sovereign state called the 'Libyan Arab
Republic' was swiftly declared. There was little opposition
even in Cyrenaica and Fezzan where the populace seemed
broadly in support, especially when the heir to the Sanusi

throne 'Prince Hassan' renounced all claims and was said to support the new regime. Within days the Revolutionary Command Council (RCC) was in control, from which the charismatic 27-year-old Colonel Muammar Gaddafi emerged as leader, stating that the 'dark ages' of the old regime and colonialism were ended. Idris never returned to Libya, and spent the rest of his life in exile in Egypt, until his death in 1983.

There were obvious similarities between this coup and the one that installed Nasser as Egyptian President in 1952. But in Libya the deeply religious Colonel Gaddafi wanted to establish a true Arab nation with Islam as the state religion. British and American bases were closed (the US Wheelus air-force base was at one time the largest outside America), banks and most of the oil industry were nationalised, and alcohol was banned.

Gaddafi: in power since 1969

Modern Libya

Gaddafi saw himself as the natural successor to Nasser, and fiercely promoted Arab unity – only to be snubbed at every attempt to establish permanent links with other Arab states. He had strong ideas of what his modern independent Islamic State would stand for, and shared his vision of the future with the publication of his *Green Book* in 1976. A cornerstone

The new Libya: a Tripoli hotel

of this 'Third Universal Theory' was the equality of the people, who would become the socialist government themselves through a series of local committees and national congresses. A year later the country was renamed the Libyan Arab Jamahiriya (State of the Masses), and embarked on a massive programme of building schools, universities and hospitals.

Vast amounts of money from oil were spent promoting the Palestinian cause from an anti-Israeli stance. This still continues today, but gone are the days of supporting radical armed groups around the world. Accusations of state-sponsored terrorism led to the imposition of an embargo by the US in 1982 and the resulting bombing of Tripoli and Benghazi by the US in 1986, which killed Gaddafi's adopted daughter among others. Further sanctions were imposed by the UN against Libya for not extraditing the suspects of the PanAm Lockerbie bombing in 1988, and the country languished in an international vacuum.

The EU eased its embargo in 1999 after the Lockerbie suspects stood trial in The Hague, but it wasn't until 2004 that widespread sanctions were lifted. The long period of isolation gave Gaddafi the opportunity to rethink the direction of Libya, and recently private enterprise has replaced state socialism. With a new emphasis directed at becoming the leading state in Africa, Libya is rapidly making up for lost time, and certainly has a lot to offer the curious visitor.

Historical Landmarks

*c.*1000BC Phoenicians and Greeks trade along North African coast.

631BC City of Cyrene founded by the Greeks.

264–146BC Three Punic wars between Carthage and Rome.

107BC Tripolitania province comes under Roman control.

74BC Rome takes Cyrenaica from the Greeks.

AD365 Large earthquake destroys most of the ancient sites.

455 After the collapse of Rome, the Vandals take control of Libya.

533 Belisarius drives out Vandals: a century of Byzantine rule.

642–63 Libya conquered by the Arabs.

890–1049 Fatimid rule, from their later capital of Cairo.

1146 Normans from Sicily invade and control the coast.

1160–1510 Hafsid dynasties of Moorish rulers.

1551–1911 Ottoman Empire controls Tripolitania.

1911 Italy invades. Start of Sanusi resistance.

1940–3 Libya is caught up in fighting between the Axis and Allies.

1949 Cyrenaica becomes an independent state, with Britain controlling Tripolitania and France the Fezzan.

1951 King Idris is granted independence by the UN.

1953 Libya joins the Arab League and two years later the UN.

1961 Oil exported for the first time.

1969 King Idris is overthrown in a coup. Colonel Muammar Gaddafi becomes head of Revolutionary Command Council.

1976 Gaddafi shares his vision of the future in his *Green Book*.

1977 Libya renamed Libyan Arab Jamahiriya (State of the Masses).

1982 Embargo imposed by US.

1986 US bombing of Tripoli and Benghazi.

1992 Sanctions imposed by UN against Libya for not extraditing suspects of Lockerbie bombing in 1988.

1999 EU embargo is eased after Libya allows Lockerbie suspects to stand trial in The Hague.

2003 UN embargo lifted. Private enterprise replaces state socialism.

2004 US and EU sanctions are lifted.

WHERE TO GO

Libya is a large country, with the majority of tourist sites on the Mediterranean coast. Highlights not to be missed are the magnificent Roman cities of Leptis Magna and Sabratha, both within easy reach of Tripoli, and the imposing Greek city of Cyrene and its harbour Apollonia, east of Benghazi. To these can be added a visit to the Jebel Nafusa (Western Mountains), south of Tripoli, and, further south, the Sahara Desert. Most visitors begin by arriving in the capital city.

TRIPOLI

Central **Tripoli**, known locally as Ṭarābulus, is a surprisingly ◄ small and relatively quiet city, and easy to walk around in a day. With Green Square (Assaha al-Khadrah) at the centre, the area to the west is the old walled city, known as the Medina, dominated by the Red Castle (As-Serai al-Hamra), which today houses the Antiquities Department and the National Museum *(see page 28)*. Modern Tripoli lies to the south and east, along the roads radiating from Green Square. The city is an intriguing mix of North Africa, Oriental Islam and decaying imperial Mediterranean grandeur – with a hint of Classical Rome thrown in for good measure.

> **The name Tripoli and the Arabic version, Ṭarābulus, are both derived from the Greek Tripolitania or 'Three Cities'** *(see page 14).*

The city owes its importance to its position: the meeting point of three important Saharan caravan trading routes, from Sudan, Chad and Niger. It was only after the Arab conquest in the 7th century that the name Tripoli came into use, when the Arabs chose ancient

UNESCO-protected Leptis Magna

Oea as their main centre. Virtually no Roman antiquities remain visible in the city today, but it does mean that Sabratha and Leptis Magna have been left virtually untouched for us to enjoy today.

The National Museum

The impressive fortified Red Castle has always been the centre of control for Tripoli's rulers, and today houses Tripoli's **National Museum**, a spectacular collection of Phoenician, Greek and Roman artefacts (open Tues–Sun 9am–1pm and 3–6pm; admission fee). Even though the museum is not large by international stan-

Part of the Four Seasons mosaic in the National Museum

dards, a guided tour will highlight the important exhibits. Immediately inside is a fine **Statue of Venus** from the Hadrianic Baths at Leptis, and on the wall behind is a complex mosaic of fish and gladiatorial battles taken from the Dar Buk Ameera Roman villa in Zliten. Just opposite these is a complete Libyan-Roman tomb from the Ghirza region. Impossible to miss, and slightly out of step with the timeline, is a colourful Volkswagen Beetle, used by Colonel Gaddafi leading up to the revolution.

The main collection in Gallery 9 is split into two sections – one for Leptis, the other for Sabratha. Models show how the crowded cities would have looked – impressions to carry with you when visiting the sites. From both sites there are stunning intricate floor mosaics, finely carved statues and details of colossal temples. In the corner of the Leptis room, next to the superb **Four Seasons mosaic**, also from the Villa Dar Buk Ameera, is the fascinating statue of **Artemis of Ephesus**, her multiple breasts a sign of fertility. Rooms leading from here contain important finds from Cyrene.

On the first floor, Gallery 11 features details of the original carvings on the Arch of Septimius Severus at Leptis, with other rooms dedicated to later Roman and Byzantine rule. The second floor covers the Islamic period in Libya, with emphasis on architecture, and full-size rooms from houses in Ghadames and Tripoli.

The third floor explores folkloric themes from around the country with traditional dress and household items. The fourth floor is dedicated to Libyan independence and usually closed. Not all galleries are continuously open, and access to the attractive outside courtyards, battlements and viewpoints is restricted. For security, bags must be deposited at the left-luggage counter immediately inside the entrance.

Mosaics

A wide variety of decorated floors and pavements are found in Punic and Roman towns, ranging from elaborate floral and geometric designs to simple utilitarian floors. Mosaics are made from small cubes of stone called tesserae, ranging in size from 0.5cm to 2cm (⅕-¾in). Marble, limestone, terracotta (baked clay) and even glass were used, usually in two bedding layers. The most common types are monochrome (using either black or white tesserae), bichrome (normally black and white) and polychrome (two or more colours) and are usually Roman or later.

The Old City (Medina)

To enter the Medina through the main gateway from Green Square is to glimpse what it was like centuries ago. Since Roman times, the city has frequently been rebuilt, and most of the buildings to be seen today date from the 16th century. These include the main mosques, *souqs* and the traditional overnight caravanserais (*fonduqs*) for traders who continue to bring their goods from the depths of the Sahara. Immediately inside the Bab al-Manshiya (Gateway of the New Suburb) you can go straight ahead or turn first left (up the Souq al-Attara, described below). The great thing is that the Medina is not so large as to get you lost, and whichever direction you take, you will soon find yourself back in the modern world.

A bridal shop in the Medina

The street ahead, **Souq al-Mushir** (Marshal's Market), has glittering displays of gold and silverware, colourful bridal shops, and everything from miniature perfumes to giant suitcases which stretch away to the Ottoman clock tower in the distance.

The building located behind the pillared archway to the left is the **Jama Ahmed Pasha Karamanli** (Karamanli Mosque). Though the largest mosque inside the Medina, this mid-18th-century domed building still retains an air of intimacy for worshippers who pray amid the forest of marble columns.

The walls are covered in colourful geometric patterned tiles, and the ceiling is decorated by delicate stucco in North African style. The roots of the Karamanli dynasty that ruled Tripoli for over a century can be seen in the octagonal minaret and their tombs, which have carved Turkish head-dresses atop the tombstone. Even if you cannot

Metalwork at the Souq al-Ghizdir

enter the mosque, you can peek a view at the prayer hall and the tombs if the doorway is open.

At the end of the street the traditional teahouse opposite the clock tower is a great place for a break in your Medina tour. Enter the narrow alleyway to the left of this tower into the **Souq al-Ghizdir** (Copper Market), a hive of noisy metalwork activity producing plates, bowls, urns, trinkets, and the large metal crescents to be placed at the top of minarets. At the end of this alley turn left and left again into the wide **Souq al-Turk** (Turkish Market), with many shops. At the end, turn left to rejoin the first street you walked along. Turn right around the Karamanli Mosque back towards the main entrance gate, the Bab al-Manshiya. Turn right at the end of the mosque into the bustling **Souq al-Attara** (Spice Market), with many popular gold shops, made busier by the myriad street traders who rush off with their goods at the first sight of a policeman.

To the left and running parallel to this street is an alleyway of carpet-sellers and a small courtyard of antiques traders. Souq al-Attara turns right at the end, but notice two things: the steps to the left leading to the small Souq al-Siagha (Goldsmith's Market), and, straight ahead, the restored Fonduq Bir Zekry,

The minaret of the Druj Mosque

an old caravanserai resting place for overland traders, their animals and goods. It is now home to a busy tea-house and a few souvenir shops located in the former overnight rooms.

The right turn becomes Souq al-Siagha, with more gold and jewellery shops. First left is Trigh al-Helga, which leads to clothes shops, a hidden restored *fonduq* on the left, now selling crafts, and the local lunchtime restaurant al-Burei on the right (up steps just between two arches that cross the street). The fruit-and-vegetable sellers are at the end.

Returning and continuing along Souq al-Siagha, the entrance on the left leads to the covered **textile *souq***, selling clothing and materials. After 100m (100 yards) the street wriggles left and right around two mosques. On the left is the Jama an-Naga (Mosque of the She-Camel), whose foundations are said to belong to the first mosque in Tripoli, even though the current building, with its unusual square minaret, dates from the early 17th century. The small Sufi mosque on the right with its minaret hanging out over the street is the Zawiat Sidi abd al-Qader. Continue past these two mosques to the Jama al-Kharruba (Mosque of the Carob Tree) on the left, said to have been built on the site of the last carob tree, stripped bare by sufferers of the plague looking for its medicinal properties.

Turn left at the end, and after 50m (55 yards) is the Sharia Jama ad-Draghut. Turn right and notice the minaret of the **Druj Mosque** on the right overhanging the street at the narrowest section. Continue along this busy thoroughfare to the 'four Roman columns' crossroads, so named because of the re-used ancient columns on the corners of the buildings. The final house that you have just passed on the left is the famous **Dar Karamanli** (Yusuf Karamanli House; open Tues–Sun 9am–1.30pm; admission fee). Many of these buildings built by wealthy families around 200 years ago had fallen into disrepair, but some have fortunately been saved.

The basic design of an open courtyard surrounded by colonnades and balconies is similar to some of the Roman villas excavated along the coast. Extra elements include the Arab love of water, with a central fountain, and colourful tile-work on the lower walls, with Turkish designs. Inside the rooms are displays of traditional dress, period furniture, musical instruments and other items showing the wealth of this Turkish family that once ruled Tripoli.

Colourful tiles on the walls of the Dar Karamanli

If you turn left at the Roman columns crossroads you can proceed along the narrow street to arrive at the lively taxi and bus station area around Bab al-Jedid (New Gate) not far from the Corinthia Hotel. Turning right at the Roman columns crossroads would take you down to the seafront, but continuing straight ahead brings you to an open crossroads, the Place des Nazaréens. Situated to the left is the restored Banca di Roma building, and ahead is the old bookshop. The small square to the left contains the old Turkish prison on the right and the former Catholic cathedral of Santa Maria degli Angeli on the left, immediately behind the Banca di Roma.

With the Banca di Roma behind you, walk down the road towards the sea, past the high blank walls of the Othman Pasha Mosque and *madrasa* (school) on the left, to the Jama ad-Draghut (Draghut Mosque) on the right. Named after a

This restored house is now home to the Yahzarkom Arts Centre

notorious pirate and governor of Tripoli in the mid-
16th century, this extensive
building contains a pillared
prayer hall, a *hammam*
(Turkish bath), tombs and
two courtyards with a circular minaret. It belongs to an
earlier Turkish style, which

**Three common symbols
that supposedly ward
off evil can be seen
everywhere, from gold
charms and amulets
to painted images: the
Hand of Fatima, a fish
and an animal horn.**

has been reconstructed after damage in World War II. The
gateway at the end of the street now has a splendid pair of
metal decorated doors.

From here turn left to get fine views of the fishing boats in
the harbour. Along this waterfront is another well-restored
house, now the Yahzarkom Arts Centre. The isolated white
building on the right is the Sheikh Sidi Abdul Wahab
Mosque, named after a holy man of the early 14th century
who is buried here. Libyans making pilgrimage to Mecca
traditionally say their final prayers here before leaving.

About 100m (100 yards) inland is the only substantial
relic of Roman Oea, the **Arch of Marcus Aurelius** (open all
the time, free) which once welcomed visitors arriving at the
old port. Dedicated to the co-emperors Marcus Aurelius and
Lucius Verus in AD163, today this heavy square archway of
carved stone appears to be sunken, but this was the original
level of the ground at the road junction of the Cardo and the
Decumanus. The triumphal arch was a small part of the
forum, and, intriguingly, undisturbed Roman ruins must lie
buried at this level under most of the Medina.

The story of the arch's survival is interesting, as it has
been a storehouse, stable, public house, shop and even a
cinema – essential establishments at various times over two
millennia. The great wealth of Oea is indicated by the fact
that the arch was completely covered in marble, and carvings

The traditional *nargile* pipe

of the two deities of the city, Apollo and Minerva, can be still be seen. Some of the carved blocks on display around the edge of the arch are remains of a nearby Roman temple.

Looking back towards the sea from the arch, the building with colonnaded archways on the left, behind locked gates, is the former Italian resthouse.

Located directly opposite on the right-hand side is the **Old French Consulate** (open Tues–Sun 9am–1.30pm; admission fee), on the corner of the small street leading away from the arch (which will take you back to the Place des Nazaréens). This restored ornate building with central courtyard and colonnaded galleries dates from 1630, and was the home of the French representative for more than 300 years.

Continuing away from the sea, the large green doors at the end of this street belong to the **Gurgi Mosque** (Georgia Mosque), whose slender twin-balconied minaret is the tallest in the Medina. Turn right and immediately left up Sharia al-Kuwash (Baker's Street), and the entrance to the mosque is on the left. It was built in the 1830s by a wealthy corsair named Mustafa (who captured ships on behalf of the ruling Karamanli family) from Georgia in Eastern Europe. At the end of the marble-column prayer hall is the delicately carved *mihrab* (niche direction to Mecca) behind which is the *madrasa*. On the right is the *minbar* (Islamic pulpit), and behind this are the tombs of Mustafa and his family.

Further up Sharia al-Kuwash and just after the first left turn behind the Gurgi Mosque is another restored house, which was the **Old British Consulate** (open Tues–Sun 9am–1.30pm; admission fee). A plaque on the wall gives information on what is now called Dar Nuwayji. It was built in 1744 for the Karamanli family and offered to the British, who used it until the 1920s. There are wonderful views from the roof terrace across the Gurgi Mosque to the modern harbour. Just opposite is an old house called ad-Dar, recently converted into dining rooms, also with great views on a summer evening from the roof terrace *(see az-Zareeq, page 139)*. Back on Sharia al-Kuwash, look up a narrow street opposite for a view of the white minaret of the Sidi Salem Mosque.

Continuing up Sharia al-Kuwash you arrive at another crossroads. Ahead will take you through a lively residential area of the Medina and eventually down steps under the old walls to face the Corinthia Hotel. But turning left and then left again after some 100m (100 yards) will bring you back to the Place des Nazaréens.

The New City

Across Green Square directly opposite the Medina gateway is the Salim Café, hidden under some arches. The road leading away on

Islamic Arts and Crafts School

the left is Sharia Mohammed al-Magharief, and the one to the right is Sharia 1 September (1 September Street). Taking the left street, follow Sharia Mohammed al-Magharief away from Green Square. One block along on the right is the spacious **Galleria de Bono** arched plaza, giving some idea of the grandeur during Italian times. Continuing up this main shopping street for about 500m (550 yds) will bring you into Maydan al-Jazayir (Algeria Square). The white building ahead is the main post office, and to the right is the imposing façade of the modern Roman Catholic cathedral, now converted into a mosque. Immediately on the right are some cafés and restaurants, and to the left is another open piazza with teahouse, popular with *nargile* water-pipe smokers.

A short-cut through to 1 September Street is to go to the right of the old cathedral, but to see the former People's Palace continue straight ahead uphill. This beautiful yellow-domed, white building set in its own (now neglected) grounds was constructed in 1931 and is now the **National Library**, making more functional use of the banquet rooms and glass-domed central courtyard as study areas. To the north on the left the al-Dahra district stretches towards the port, including several hotels and the San Francisco Catholic Church. With the library ahead, turn right onto the main road and first right onto the pleasant tree-lined 1 September Street.

Midway back to Green Square on the left, opposite the Galaxy Restaurant, is the long yellow façade of the Andalusian flavoured **Islamic Arts and Crafts School**. Established in 1898, it was the first foundation for education, and many disciplines still continue here. Further down on the left look out for the useful Dar Fergiani Bookshop *(see page 101)* and just beyond that the interesting Ghadames Art Gallery *(see page 101),* which represents many local working artists. Opposite this is the other façade of the Galleria de Bono.

LEPTIS MAGNA

Recently restored: the Triumphal Arch of Septimius Severus

The Roman city of **Leptis Magna**, 125km (78 miles) east of Tripoli, is a World Heritage site and one of the highlights of a visit to Libya. Most of the archaeological site (open daily 8am–5pm; admission fee) has been well protected by a covering of sand for over one thousand years, and a better understanding of the layout is helped by the restoration work of the Italians over the last century. It should be noted that only about a third of the ancient city is uncovered, and even the extent of the Roman city inland is undetermined, due to modern buildings to the east of al-Khoms (al-Khums) city. The origins of the name Leptis are uncertain, but the Romans called it Magna to distinguish it from Leptis Minor, further along the coast (now in Tunisia).

The site was first developed in the 6th century BC as a coastal trading post around the reef-protected mouth of Wadi Labda, by seafaring Phoenician traders from the eastern Mediterranean. Following the defeat of the Phoenicians in the Third Punic War in 146BC, local desert tribes eyed the site enviously, but new Roman fortifications and a buffer zone of fortified farms on the fertile soil protected the important harbour and trading centre for hundreds of years. Its location increased in importance through grain and olive production and the expanding trans-Saharan desert trade, bringing exotic goods from West and Central Africa such as wild animals, slaves and gold to Rome and the rest of the empire.

The Triumphal Gateway

During the 2nd century AD the city reached its peak of prosperity when the Libyan Septimius Severus became emperor and spared no expense in glorifying and expanding his hometown of 80,000 inhabitants. Details celebrating his life are shown in magnificent splendour on the recently restored **Triumphal Arch of Septimius Severus**, which is the first monument to be seen. It stands at the main road junction of the Decumanus (running east–west from Alexandria in Egypt through to Oea, Sabratha and eventually Carthage) and the Cardo Maximus, which connected to the fortified farms, a Roman milestone indicating the distance involved, about 70km (45 miles). The arch was erected in AD203 to commemorate Severus' return, and is decorated with carved marble panels, the originals of which are now on display at the National Museum in Tripoli. The southern frieze shows the emperor shaking hands with his eldest son Caracalla.

Lucius Septimius Severus Pertinax

The only African to attain the position of emperor, Septimius Severus was born at Leptis in AD146, and became a Roman senator at age 30. He seized the imperial throne in 193, after a period of civil war and anarchy. During his reign he expanded the army, increased their pay, and also committed funds to the expansion of both Leptis and Carthage (in present-day Tunisia). One reason for his popularity could be his abolition of taxes in these cities. He died of disease at Eboracum (York) in 211 and was succeeded as emperor by his son Caracalla.

The impressive Hadrianic Baths date from the 2nd century AD

Turn right at the arch and proceed down the Decumanus, paved with limestone blocks. At the end, note the carved phallic symbol (in this instance a winged penis) embedded high up on the left wall. Such symbols not only warded off evil, but were also a representation of Bacchus, the deity of the city. Turn left until you enter an open inner-city sports area, called the Palaestra (literally 'a place for wrestling'), used for gymnastics exercises, originally surrounded by a covered portico.

The extensive ruins to the right are what remains of the impressive **Hadrianic Baths**, built beside Wadi Labda. The vast and orderly complex consists of linked rooms used for public bathing – the *natatio* (cool swimming pool), *frigidarium* (cold chamber), *tepidarium* (warm chamber), *caldarium* (hot bath) and finally the *laconica* (sweat room) which leads directly back to the *frigidarium*. Begun in the time of Hadrian around AD126, the baths were continually modernised over the following 100 years, and contained many beautiful carved statues that are now housed in the National Museum. Returning to the Palaestra, note the communal marble latrines on the right.

Severan Leptis

Behind these further to the right are the remains of the **Nymphaeum**, a shrine for Nymph worship. The massive rear wall collapsed backwards in the earthquake of AD365, revealing that it was faced with marble but mainly built of concrete, a Roman invention of lime mortar, sand, water and small stones (known as *caementa*).

The **colonnaded street** ran from the baths to the harbour, a distance of over 400m (440yds), flanked on both sides by porticoes with 125 huge cipollino columns.

Through the jumble of scattered carved blocks on the left is an entrance into the monumental area known as the **Severan**

The Severan Forum is surrounded by heads of Medusa

Forum, which represents the might and opulence of this city's social centre. To the left is a giant podium with staircase that supports the remnants of a temple dedicated to the emperor's family. From this lofty position, the massive blocks of masonry and split columns that litter the floor look like an

Liber Pater was a name used to represent the god of wine Bacchus (Dionysus), particularly in poetry. Bacchus and Hercules were the two protective gods of the city of Leptis Magna and also of the Leptis-born emperor Septimius Severus.

impossible building-block puzzle for the archaeologists. Surrounding the open courtyard, measuring 100m x 60m (325ft x 195ft), are imposing walls with Doric friezes. The columns of the porticoes carry arches, between which are charismatic Medusa heads. A short series of these arches have been rebuilt at ground level over to the right.

At the far end of the forum, walk through into the adjoining **Severan Basilica**, which served as a justice court. This ◄ impressive building is divided lengthwise by two rows of columns into a nave, with side aisles formerly of two storeys supporting a wooden roof. At each end is a half-domed apse, framed by intricately carved three-sided pilasters depicting the Labours of Hercules and Liber Pater, as well as satyrs and musicians. Notice that the ends were built of brickwork (like the rear of the Nymphaeum), which made it much easier to construct the desired curved walls. During the reign of Justinian in the 6th century, this was converted into a Byzantine church, as can be seen by the small pulpit on the floor of the nave.

Exiting the northwestern end, walk away from the colonnaded road and around to inspect the Byzantine walls, hurriedly erected by reusing fallen blocks to protect a much reduced city from increasing tribal desert raids.

The Old Forum

Ionic capital in the Old Forum

The site now opens up with the remains of the **Old Forum** ahead and the harbour over to the far right. The Old Forum was situated at the coastal end of the Cardo Maximus, and is a collection of several interesting buildings: the Curia (Municipal Senate House) and Old Basilica to the right, two temples (Hercules and Liber Pater) on the left and the Old Forum Church (formerly Temple of Trajan) behind. Walk around some recent excavations of earlier Phoenician buildings en route to the northern wall of the silted harbour, to see the base of the old northern lighthouse, built in the style of the Pharos in Alexandria.

Retrace your steps and skirt round the two temples close to the sea: there are three enormous granite cipollino columns, looted from the Hadrianic Baths at the end of the 17th century by the French Consul. It is said that they were destined for the palace at Versailles, near Paris, but this is as far they got.

Heading inland towards the theatre, the small Serapeum (Temple of Serapis) is dedicated to an earlier Egyptian god, indicating strong links with Alexandria. This is thought to be one of the oldest parts of the city, as the general population in Roman times remained deeply attached to their Punic roots. Four statues from this site are now in the Leptis Museum.

The Market and Theatre

Standing above this is the **Market**, which was begun around 9BC, and consists of two almost identical *tholoi* (kiosks) with serving counters and marble measuring-blocks for liquids, grains and materials. Two arches now cross the Cardo, the first dedicated to Tiberius, the second to Trajan. To the right of the Arch of Trajan is the large area of the Chalcidicum with porticoes and booths, whose exact purpose is still to be determined, but which was possibly an extension to the market.

Inscriptions at the doorway of the 8,000-seat **Theatre** indicate that it was constructed at the same time as the market and paid for by the same man, Annobal Rufus. Built with limestone blocks, it has withstood the elements of two millennia better than Sabratha's theatre, which was constructed from sandstone. As well as giving excellent sight of the *pulpitum* (stage) and three-storey *scaenae frons* (stage wall), there are commanding

Modern theatregoers look down on the 1st-century stage

views to the sea and across the entire site from the top of the *cavea* (auditorium). This top tier originally had a portico which contained a small temple to the goddess Ceres, whose giant statue is now in the National Museum. The extent of the pre-Roman city was confirmed when Phoenician tombs were found under the stage area during reconstruction. This earlier Phoenician city is thought to be roughly 2m (6½ft) below the Roman site.

Returning to the Cardo and turning right will bring you back to the Severan Arch. From here there is a walk of almost 1km (½ mile) via the West Gate (further along the Decumanus) to reach the multi-chambered Hunting Baths, so called because of the painted frescoes inside the domed rooms which depict the hunting of lions as well as more tranquil Nile scenes. Unfortunately, they are often closed to the public, but it is a pleasant, if arduous, walk along a sandy track down to the beach.

Located at the entrance to the main site is the **Museum** (open Tues–Sun 8am–6pm; admission fee), which houses some fine objects and has good information in English. The story of Libya's prehistory and how the first small seasonal Phoenician settlement turned into a wealthy Roman city is all overseen by a giant cut-out figure of a waving Colonel Gaddafi. There are also examples from outlying sites such as the impressive Villa Silene and the area of Ghirza.

As if all this were not enough to make Leptis Magna one of the most impressive Roman sites in the world, there is more to be seen along the coast to the east.

Eastern Sites

The best view of the **Old Harbour** is found by walking along the eastern wall past warehouses, moorings and steps to a small Doric temple that complemented the lighthouse on the opposite harbour wall. Later fortifications were from Byzantine times, when the harbour needed to be defended, even though it was silting up badly by then.

Further around the coast, and situated far enough away from the city so as not to be heard, is the magnificent **Amphitheatre** (open daily 8am–6pm; admission fee), built during the time of Nero (AD54–68). Almost complete, this elliptical stadium of public entertainment stands majestically overlooking the sea, and certainly witnessed some mighty gladiatorial contests to the death between man and beast, cheered on by an estimated crowd of around 16,000.

The celebrated statue of multi-breasted Artemis of Ephesus, now in the National Museum, was found here, and probably rested in a small temple built at the top of the auditorium. Down at beach level between the Amphitheatre and the sea is the enormous overgrown **Circus**, built about a century later and now needing a bit of imagination to bring it to life. The racetrack originally had starting gates, with semicircular bends at each end and seating for over 20,000 people.

The devastating earthquake of AD365 hastened the decline of Roman power, and Leptis suffered greatly at the hands of the Vandals during the first half of the 5th century. The end of Leptis Magna came when the Byzantines finally lost out to the attacks of local tribes. Within 100 years, when the Arabs arrived in 643, the city was already a sand-covered ruin, ripe for plunder by every invader.

The well-preserved Amphitheatre was built under the reign of Nero

Excursions from Leptis

Eight Roman villas belonging to wealthy citizens have been discovered along the coast either side of Leptis Magna, and the remains of many more are undoubtedly yet to be found. Most are covered with sand and well protected for security, but a few have been excavated and provide the fine displays of mosaics in the National and Leptis museums. Much of this coastline is within military areas, but it may be possible to get permission to visit Villa Silene and Villa Dar Buk Ameera.

➤   **Villa Silene** (open daily with permission 8am–6pm; admission fee), located a few kilometres west of al-Khoms, was discovered only in 1974, and has recently been restored. Decorations dating from the 2nd century AD cover 800 sq metres (8,600 sq ft) inside and out, where expansive terraces look out across the beach and coast, similar to the Seaward Baths at Sabratha. An open three-sided courtyard is decorated

Dar Buk Ameera mosaics lightly covered by sand for protection

with more than 150 colourful mosaics of interlocking circles, knots, cubes, interlaced cables, wheels and spirals. Inside the many beautiful rooms are more incredibly fine mosaics showing races in the hippodrome and gladiatorial scenes.

On the other side of Leptis is the **Villa Dar Buk Ameera** (no guardian on site, opened with permission) on the seafront at Zliten. The site has been excavated but not restored, with the external mosaics covered by sand. There is not much for visitors to see beyond the low walls separating the rooms that once held the interior mosaics, now in the National Museum.

In the town centre of **Zliten** (Zlīṭan) is the impressive **Mausoleum of Imam Abdul Salem**, who died in the 16th century, when Zliten was an important Islamic city. His reputation came from his success as an arbitrator between warring tribes in the Villa Silene area, and there has since been a tradition of visiting his tomb. Next to the mausoleum is a *madrasa*, a religious place of learning. Further east along the coast is **Misrata** (Miṣrātah), Libya's third-largest city, mainly of Italian colonial design and relatively quiet and orderly. Recent port expansion and nearby heavy industry has greatly enlarged the city.

The area of **Ghirza** south of Misrata has many examples of ancient Libyan monumental tombs dating from before the 5th century AD. Some are obelisk tombs, similar to the Punic tomb at Sabratha, while others are small temple tombs, usually two or three storeys built of limestone. These were erected in remote areas along the Roman frontier. One of the easiest to visit is at **as-Senama** (open all the time, free) on the road from Gharyan to Tarhuna (Tarhūnah); it has Corinthian pilasters on a square podium with a false door. The carvings are well preserved, and the whole structure rests above a subterranean tomb chamber. There are examples of these tombs in the museums at Tripoli, Leptis and also **Bani Walid**, a modern town and good base for visiting these and the more southerly sites.

SABRATHA

Modern Sabratha lies 65km (40 miles) west of Tripoli along the main coastal highway, and the site itself (open daily 8am–5.30pm; admission fee) is reached via a 1.5-km (1-mile) link road. To help you spot it, the world's tallest minaret is being constructed beside the main road. Like Leptis Magna and Oea (present-day Tripoli), this city owes its beginnings to early Phoenician traders who used the small natural harbour en route to the Iberian peninsula. The origins of the name are uncertain, but it could have meant 'grain market'. In contrast to the immensity and grandeur of Leptis, this site is more delicate and spacious, as befits the birthplace of an emperor's wife (Flavia Domitilla, wife of Vespasian). Ancient **Sabratha** had an estimated population of 35,000, but with no triumphal arches was considered less important than Leptis Magna, which had five.

Sabratha's wonderfully restored Roman Theatre once seated 5,000

The Theatre

Approaching the entrance to the **Theatre** is a Peristyle House, the villa of a wealthy family built in the 2nd century AD with fine mosaics and a sunken corridor. The spectacular Theatre was beautifully restored by a series of Italian archaeologists between the world wars, and has regularly been used to stage modern productions since 1937. Originally built of sandstone, many sections of the *cavea* (auditorium) are

The Three Graces at the Theatre

now missing, but are thought to have seated 5,000 spectators. However, it is the towering 25-m (80-ft), three-storey *scaenae frons* (stage wall), consisting of 108 Corinthian columns, that gives the theatre a real presence. One of the main features is the marble relief figures decorating the front of the stage. In a bay on the left are the Nine Muses and to the right the Three Graces. Between them are poised dancers, scenes from plays, comic and tragic masks, and popular gods and goddesses. Behind the stage are rooms for actors and scenery that are still in use today.

The Eastern City

Walk towards the sea to see the monuments of the eastern part of the city stretching along the coast to the right, starting with the foundations of the Temple of Hercules on the Decumanus, the main east-west road. Nearer to the sea are the **Christian Basilicas**, with remains of a semicircular apse, baptistery and some extensive mosaics, dating from the 4th century but

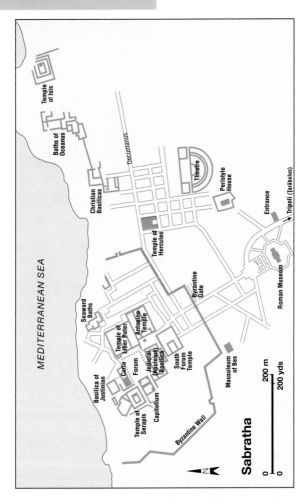

MEDITERRANEAN SEA

Temple of Isis

Baths of Oceanus

Decumanus

Christian Basilicas

Theatre

Peristyle House

Temple of Hercules

Entrance

Tripoli (Tarābulus)

Seaward Baths

Byzantine Gate

Roman Museum

Basilica of Justinian

Temple of Liber Pater

Antonine Temple

Curia

Forum

Judicial Apulejus Basilica

South Forum Temple

Temple of Serapis

Capitolium

Mausoleum of Bes

Byzantine Wall

Sabratha

N

0   200 m
0   200 yds

probably converted from an earlier bathing complex.

Another 100m (110yds) further on are the **Baths of Oceanus**, a small bathing area with chambers off to the sides. The floor of the bath was once covered in a fabulous mosaic design with a central hexagon featuring the head of a sea god, which is now inside the site museum. The columns up a slight hill belong to the **Temple of Isis**, dating from the 1st century AD. Fragments of a statue of Isis uncovered here are

Corinthian columns at the Temple of Isis

also now in the site museum. The oblong central courtyard was surrounded by porticoes of Corinthian columns. Sandstone erosion, coastal subsidence and Byzantine rebuilding have all affected the structure, but the remains are impressive, overlooking the sea and the eastern end of the city. Away from the city, as at Leptis, are the remains of an amphitheatre some 1km (½ mile) further east along the coast and 250m (275yds) inland, but many sections are foundations only.

The Western City

Heading west back along the Decumanus to the main site, you enter the western half of the city. This was the original Roman town built on Phoenician ruins; it expanded eastwards, only to shrink back within the defensive walls of the Byzantines. The most commanding position in this area is to the right of the Cardo, from the podium of the **Antonine Temple**. In front of the temple is a courtyard with steps leading up to the porch, which originally had six Corinthian columns. Inscriptions on the architrave between these columns ascribes the temple to Marcus Aurelius and Lucius Verus around AD168. Fragments of animal bones found here suggest a similarity with the *tophet* in Carthage as a place of sacrifice.

Across the piazza, opposite the front of the temple are two more buildings, the South Forum Temple of unknown dedication to the left, and the **Judicial (Apuleius) Basilica** to the right. This current church dates from around AD440, but the building had an earlier life as a law-court, and takes its name from the Latin writer Apuleius of Madaura, who defended himself against charges of witchcraft here in AD157. There are great views over the basilica, which is similar to the Severan Basilica at Leptis, from the top of the unexcavated mound behind the apse to the west.

Heading towards the sea, the **Forum** is a large open space at one time completely paved with metamorphic limestone, situated here so that goods arriving at the port could be handled easily. It originally consisted of market stalls, but the shops became more permanent as neighbouring large monuments

Mosaic Craftsmen

Mosaic makers used compasses, rulers and stylets for geometrical shapes. Owners could choose set designs from templates, with the colour affecting the cost depending on where the *tesserae* were sourced. Mosaic making was generally considered a lowly profession, apart from the *pictor imaginarius* – the chief draughtsman who designed and constructed the most intricate central details. Apprentices and those less skilled completed the fill-in and plain backgrounds. Although individual works were attributed to a particular craftsman in the Hellenistic period, the artists who made the finest mosaics in Roman times remain uncredited and unknown.

were subsequently constructed around the space. At the western end of the Forum is the **Capitolium** or Temple of Jupiter, dedicated to the triad of Jupiter, Juno and Minerva.

Opposite this at the eastern end of the Forum is the late-1st-century **Temple of Liber Pater** with its restored Corinthian columns, originally with fluted shafts. Inside the podium you can see the remains of an earlier house built on the site, covered by a smaller temple built in the early 1st century. Just to the right of the entrance is a headless statue, possibly of Flavius Tullus, at one of the many fountains.

Mosaic floor at the Seaward Baths

At the rear of this temple are the **Seaward Baths** (or Forum Baths), the largest bathing complex in the city. A lot of the foundations have suffered from sea erosion, but the mosaics that remain are of exquisite colour and quality, on what is now a terrace overlooking the seashore.

Just beside the baths are communal latrines, and then continuing further west is the **Curia** (Municipal Senate House) and the **Basilica of Justinian**, nearer the sea. As a building, the basilica is an odd mixture of styles and sizes of reused blocks from other fallen buildings, but its importance is for the magnificent mosaic found in the nave. This superb intricate maze of birdlife and twisting vine branches has now been removed to the site museum.

When you stand beside the Capitolium, the final building to the west is also one of the oldest, the **Temple of Serapis**. The name comes from a Serapis head found in the ruins, indicating a strong link with Alexandria. From here there are paths around the western end of the site giving grand views over the excavations, heading towards the museum via the **Punic Mausoleum of Bes** (known as Mausoleum B). This unusual tiered structure of fluted columns from pre-Roman times features three carved lions and the Egyptian god Bes as protector of the dead. All the blocks from this monument were reused in later Byzantine structures, but some of the originals have since been recovered and placed inside the museum, reached by returning to the Cardo.

There are two museums on the site, with the smaller Punic Museum often closed. The **Roman Museum** (open 8am–5.30pm Tues–Sun; admission fee) is set back in gardens behind a courtyard of statues found at the site. The main displays are of the amazing mosaics, especially that from the Basilica of Justinian. This museum has had some recent security problems and is often closed, so it is fortunate that many of the best objects are better protected inside Tripoli's National Museum.

In AD365 the city was severely damaged by the immense earthquake, and a century later the Vandals completed the destruction. Despite attempts by the Byzantines to rebuild, the city was uninhabitable by the time of the Arab conquest.

JEBEL NAFUSA AND GHADAMES

The Jebel Nafusa, or Western Mountains, are a crescent-shaped escarpment of the Saharan plateau, roughly 600m (2,000ft) high, enclosing Tripolitania and the coastal Plain of Jefara. Rainfall is heavy, but has to be retained to enable the Berber population to survive, due to the lack of underground springs. For that reason a system of hardy dry farming has developed to produce olives, palms and fruit trees. Harsh winters and dry summers have not prevented the highly

Above: the fortified Berber granary at Qasr al-Haj

independent Berbers from surviving here away from invaders and making the area their stronghold, where almost every old building has some form of defence.

Eastern Nafusa

Starting in the east is the main town of **Gharyan**, situated on the route through the mountains, some 85km (53 miles) south of Tripoli. A modern town famous for its grape production, it is also the chief pottery centre of the country, as seen by the extensive displays of pots and bowls for sale along the roadsides around the town. Interestingly, it has examples of the underground **troglodyte houses** (open daily 9am–5.30pm; admission fee) used by Berber families, cut into the solid rock, three storeys deep. For a small fee the owner will let you walk down the sloping passageway to the bottom of the large pit, open to the sky, with rooms running off this central courtyard. Cool in summer, warm in winter and almost invisible from any distance, they proved ideal accommodation for the Berbers fleeing persecution from the coast.

Fortified Berber Granaries

An interesting style of local structure unique to the Jebel Nafusa is the fortified communal storehouse. An enclosure of barrel-vaulted storerooms was built with doors facing inwards, offering a defensive wall to the outside, which gradually grew over centuries. This Berber *qasr*, or castle, had a single defendable doorway and an open space in the middle which could be used to protect the local population (and their valuable grains and foodstuffs) in times of siege. The job of trusted guardian was passed down through a single family, who unlocked the door at certain times and would know exactly how much was inside each storeroom.

The view over Jebel Nafusa from the hilltop town of Yefren

The Jebel Nafusa escarpment is heavily eroded by wadis (dry river valleys) running north and south, so a journey across the range can be described as undulating. The high rainfall has given hardy trees the opportunity to change the Libyan landscape, and there are welcome small forests around **Yefren** (Yafran), a hilltop settlement established for thousands of years. The old town is situated some way from the new centre, but the ruined houses and mosque are in a commanding position overlooking the escarpment down onto the plain. Set some way back on the corner of a new road is a real surprise, the remnants of a Jewish synagogue with Hebrew characters carved on the ceiling. The owner, whose house now incorporates it, sometimes lets visitors inside, but practically nothing is known of its history.

At the bottom of the escarpment on the edge of the Jefara Plain is **Qasr al-Haj** (open daily 8am–5.30pm; admission fee), which can easily be visited from Sabratha. This is one of the best examples of a fortified Berber granary, and dates from the 12th century when it was founded by Sheikh Abu Jatla, a local holy man. Some of the local crops, such as dried dates, grain, figs and olive oil, are still to be seen in earthenware jars in the tiny storerooms, many of which have their traditional palm-tree doors. For a wide-angle view, climb the open stairway onto the inner balcony running just below the top, and up the steps onto the roofs of the upper storey.

Not far from the top of the zigzag road up the escarpment above Qasr al-Haj is the ruined village of **Tormeisa** (open all the time, free), spectacularly built from the local stone and perched between two sheer drop-offs 500m (1,640ft) above the Jefara Plain. Total defence was achieved by digging a ditch across the neck of the outcrop and only allowing access by a removable bridge. Today the village is completely abandoned, but you can still see an old mosque, wedding room and a camel-driven olive press in an underground cavern.

The village of Tormeisa, set high above the Jefara Plain

The views are amazing, but take care on the edge of the drops, since the backs of some old houses have simply disappeared. Some of the local boys have set up a small museum, having collected many of the outdated pieces of equipment from around the site.

The main town in this area is **Jadu**, a busy farming centre but with an old town and museum dedicated to the Berber culture and lifestyle (open Tues–Sun 8am–5.30pm; admission fee).

Western Nafusa

Situated further west and just off the modern main road is the quiet town of **Kabaw**, whose old town spills down the hillside with a mosque and olive press on view. But the main attraction is the

A Berber resident of Nalut

fortified granary at the top of the hill. This one is taller and less uniform than Qasr al-Haj, and is now disused. A festival celebrating Berber traditions is held at Kabaw every year in April, and inside there is the small tomb of a local holy man.

Almost on the border with Tunisia is the village of **Nalut**, where the main road from the coast crosses Jebel Nafusa towards Ghadames. Like many Berber settlements in the mountains, it dates from around the 11th century when the Berbers were driven from the Jefara Plain. The old city (open 8am–5.30pm daily; admission fee) is located at the end of an outcrop, with the *qasr* or fortified granary at the furthest point. Access is by walking through the old streets, and you can visit an old mosque, an olive press and other ruined buildings with underground living quarters that were cool in summer and warm in winter. This *qasr* is slightly different again, as it has no central courtyard and has expanded randomly with storerooms at all heights and angles, so that the only access is along narrow alleys, between the towering structures.

Ghadames

For those visiting the Sahara for the first time, the ancient trading city of **Ghadames** (Ghadamis), on the border with both Tunisia and Algeria, is a sight not to be missed. Today new houses, shops and mosques have spread over the hillside, but it is the old city and its unique mud architecture that recall the desert caravans and a traditional way of life that only a few of the older residents can remember.

Known as the 'Pearl of the Desert', Ghadames developed at the convergence of several caravan routes, with connections into the southern Sahara and north into the lucrative markets of Tripolitania. Referring to it as Cydemus, the ancient Romans occupied the oasis around 19BC, during their big push south to quell the warlike tribes of Germa, and later it became a fortified Roman outpost. Roman ruins at **Ras al-Ghoul** (Ghost Hill) are about 7km (4 miles) north of the old town, reachable with a four-wheel-drive vehicle.

Opposite and below: aspects of the Old City of Ghadames

A guided tour of the **Old City** (open daily 8am–6pm; admission fee) by one of the inhabitants is the best way to understand the history, culture and delicate balance between man's survival and the inhospitable desert. It is only recently that people have moved away from the old houses, but for an example of true sustainability look no further than the way of life in the Old City when nothing went to waste. Local sun-baked clay bricks, lime, gypsum, palm-tree trunks and fronds were used for building, and all waste went into fertilising irrigated market gardens around the town. The site was originally chosen because of the water supply from the Ain al-Faras, the 'Spring of the Mare'. Palaeolithic and neolithic artefacts have been found, indicating that it has always been an important oasis, with perennial springs and artesian wells providing irrigation for dates, figs, apricots and garden vegetables, as well as small crops of wheat, barley and millet.

The Scottish explorer Gordon Laing took two months to reach Ghadames from Tripoli in 1826. His 13-month trek across the Sahara is one of the greatest feats of endurance of all time, when he became the first white man to reach Timbuktu. He died on the return trip, and never consummated his marriage to Emma, the beautiful daughter of the British Consul in Tripoli. His painfully slow progress was relayed back to her by the use of the desert postal system via the trading caravans.

Enter the Old City from the main road near the cemetery and pass along a few streets until submerging into the Old City proper through a series of dark passageways, only intermittently lit from vertical shafts of sunlight. A few twists and turns down side alleys and it is impossible to know which direction will take you out of the labyrinth of square sub-ways. It all seems to be underground, but is actually at ground level when you suddenly tumble out of a side door into the glare of a small garden or date plantation.

At some point during your wanderings you will come across the old mosques with narrow ablution chambers leading down to water channels. Those mosques no longer used can be visited (open all the time; free). Every now and then you will also arrive at an open square where the major 'streets' converge. Many of the inhabitants are descended from slaves, and the Old City is divided into tribal sections, split between the two main local groups, the Wasit and Walid tribes. The white-washed walls of the main square come as a welcome rest, with access to the water distribution system from the al-Qadoos niche *(see below)* built into the 15th-century Yunis mosque.

Some fine **traditional houses** of the old town are still well maintained, the locals clinging to their culture in the face of rapid development, and it should be possible to arrange a visit through your guide. Each house is itself a warren of small

---

Measuring Time by Water

In such an arid place as Ghadames, water is the key to life and a valu-able commodity to be strictly regulated by a respected local elder, known as the Na'ib. Even as late as the 1950s, each farmer paid for his supply, controlled not by volume, but by time. A bucket filled by the Na'ib from the channel leaked water through a small hole, becoming empty after about three minutes, a unit of time known as a *qadoos*. Each time the bucket emptied, a knot was tied in a palm frond to monitor the amount sent to that farmer. Nine *qadoos* was equal to a *dermaysa*. The farmers were allowed to irrigate for so many *dermaysa* or, more importantly, told to get workers ready for redirecting water to their fields when it became their turn.

rooms and passages, richly decorated in traditional red paintwork, mirrors and pots, strictly under the control of the women, who once travelled from house to house across the privacy of the rooftops. White doors decorated with small pieces of coloured cloth indicate that the owner has been on the Haj pilgrimage to Mecca. Outside the walls, take a look at the spring and water channels that irrigate the valuable gardens, still worked by the locals.

In the summer, the older men prefer their own haunts, and wander down to the cool, shady corners for a

A decorated window in Ghadames

chat, rather than suffer the heat of the newer houses. But by sunset almost all have gone, leaving the dusty tunnels to the silent swoops of bats and the distant call of the muezzin as the ghosts of a thousand years emerge from the shadows.

The **museum** (open Tues–Sun 8am–5.30pm; admission fee) is located at the top of the hill in the new town, and contains some Roman remains as well as items from everyday life in old Ghadames.

The closest that Libya gets to commercial tourism is the late-afternoon visit to see the **sunset** across the dunes. Four-wheel-drive vehicles will take groups to the foot of the dunes close to the Algerian and Tunisian border (you will need special permission and paperwork for this, but it is always granted). Most visitors climb to the top of the first ridge and wait for sunset, but a few hardy souls continue along the ridge to the highest point. Camel and horse rides are on offer, as well as campfire Bedouin tea and *tajeelah* sand-baked bread, all to the strains of local drumming and singing.

November sees the annual Ghadames International Festival, when the Old City comes briefly back to life for three days. Houses open up for music and dance, wedding celebrations and Touareg get-togethers.

CYRENAICA

Exploring Cyrenaica is completely different from visiting the Roman remains of Tripolitania. The Jebel al-Akhdar (Green Mountains) contain some of the most fertile and rugged regions of the country, providing stunning backdrops to the many historical sites. Greek Cyrene controlled the region from the 6th century BC, but after internal struggle it formed a federation of five cities known as the Pentapolis with its port Apollonia, and colonies Berenice, Tocra and Ptolemais (the port of Barce) in the 2nd century BC. Berenice has disappeared under modern Benghazi and Tocra is yet to be excavated. In

Beit Medina Takafi courtyard

an area where invaders have fought for control for centuries, the inhabitants are proud of their independence and even today consider themselves to be very different from Tripolitanians.

Benghazi

The importance of Benghazi (Banghāzī) as Libya's second city is more of a recent development, since it was the

Souq al-Jareed is Benghazi's largest and most interesting market

headquarters of Italian occupation from 1911. The coastal
settlement of Euhesperides was founded in the 6th century BC
and was later developed around the natural harbour, to become
Berenice. Before Ottoman Turkish control, the small village
took its name from a holy man, Marsa ibn-Ghazi. Turbulent
Italian rule was followed by repeated attacks and bombings
during World War II, and there is little left of any of the old
sites. Benghazi is now the main industrial and administrative
centre of eastern Libya.

The two main hotels are pleasantly situated on either side
of the 23rd July Lake. At one end is the Sports City complex,
at the other is the older city centre, squeezed alongside the
harbour and dominated by the twin domes of the former
cathedral. Here the narrow streets are alive with fashion bou-
tiques and music shops. Near by is the renovated **Beit Medina
Takafi** (open daily 8am–10pm; free), a tranquil 200-year-
old Ottoman Turkish palace. The beautiful *diwan* has an

intricately decorated dome by craftsmen from Morocco and an open courtyard with fountain. It is the new centre for the preservation of the *medina*. The old town hall is opposite the Mosque of Umar ibn-Kuttab in Freedom Square, from which there is an extensive market, **Souq al-Jareed**, stretching for a kilometre (½ mile) into the suburbs. Head to the seafront and turn right to see the old square lighthouse, like a Magrebi minaret, close to the recent excavations of the ancient city. A further 15km (9 miles) along the coast, at **Driana** (ancient Hadrianopolis), there are modern excavations that have uncovered part of the Roman coastal road that ran from Alexandria to Carthage. There is also a small Commonwealth War Cemetery 5km (3 miles) south of the city.

Medinat Sultan

According to a legend, in order to avoid a war, the border between Greek Cyrenaica and Punic Carthage was to be settled by pairs of runners. Each pair left their home city and ran towards the other, the border agreed at wherever they met. The brothers from Carthage must have been superhumanly fit, as they managed to run more than double the distance before meeting the runners from Cyrene. The Greeks suspected foul play, and wanted the race rerun unless the brothers offered their lives after both professed their innocence. On behalf of Carthage the brothers gave up their lives to ensure that the greater share of the territory was theirs. They were honoured as the Philaeni brothers ('lovers of praise'), and their graves became the border. In the 1930s the Italians remembered them when they erected a memorial arch to celebrate completion of the coastal highway. (While passing the site during the war, British troops referred to it as 'Marble Arch'.) Giant statues of the brothers remain in awkward poses, and broken fragments of the arch lie around the field, dismantled after the 1969 revolution.

Excursions from Benghazi

A long way from Benghazi towards Sirte (Surt), the curious site of **Medinat Sultan** (Marble Arch; open daily 8am–5.30pm; admission fee) is a modern version of an ancient story *(see box opposite)*. In a field beside the road are slabs of carved stone showing fanciful details of the Italian occupation, all that remain of a 1930s triumphal arch.

One of the Philaeni brothers, commemorated by the Italians

Further east along the Gulf of Sirte is the factory producing the pipes for the Great Man-Made River Project and the towns of al-Ageila and Ajdabiya, strategic positions during the fast-moving battlefront of World War II.

Ptolemais

Roughly 100km (60 miles) east along the coast from Benghazi is **Ptolemais** (open daily 8am–5.30pm; admission fee), named after Ptolemy III, who expanded an earlier Hellenistic mercantile city. As one of the Pentapolis cities, its importance increased following Roman control over Cyrenaica, and the population enjoyed a high standard of living. Inside the small but interesting **museum** (open Tues–Sun 8am–5.30pm; admission fee) are some of the best-recovered pieces from the site, including a beautiful statue of Venus from the 2nd century AD and a wall mosaic of Orpheus taming the beasts. The mosaics in the central room are superb, especially the famous Medusa head inside an amazing geometric pattern, and

The impressive House of the Columns at Ptolemais

the Four Seasons above a pair of female tigers. There are sections of intricate mosaic work (some tiles as small as 1mm x 4mm) from a larger piece featuring fish and cockerels.

Armed with this information, you can take the long walk along the Cardo and try to make sense of the sprawling site, which has hardly been excavated at all. At the intersection of the Decumanus are some fallen Roman arches and spiral-fluted columns, and further on the left is a small theatre or Odeon for music, possibly converted into a water feature in Roman times. West from here towards the Tocra Gate is the **Villa of the Four Seasons** (the mosaic was found here), and close by is the Byzantine Church, still covered with debris protecting the domed apse. The raised platform further inland started as a Greek agora or gymnasium and later became the Roman Forum, but the real interest is what lies below. A series of giant interconnected **cisterns** retained vast amounts of water in times of need. Working across to the east you will find the impressive **House of the Columns**, where most of the best mosaics were uncovered, some still in situ. The extent and luxury of the house indicates that it belonged to the Governor or a very wealthy inhabitant. Directly opposite is an exposed double cistern from later times, and further away to the northeast is the chaotic jumble of ruins of the large fortress. After walking around the site, there is nothing better than grabbing a quick sea swim, where you can be hidden from onlookers by the pier.

Jebel al-Akhdar

The main city in the 'Green Mountains' region is **al-Bayda**, a busy working centre with a university and light industry; 40km (25 miles) west of al-Bayda is the small but fascinating site of **Qasr Libya** (open daily 8am–5.30pm; admission fee) a 6th-century Byzantine fort and church, which once held the episcopal seat of the Christian pentapolis. A floor of 50 stunning **mosaic panels** was discovered in 1957, and they are now housed in the purpose-built museum. In almost perfect condition, they are a unique collection of great importance, showing us the date the church was built (translating to AD539–40) and among other things how the Pharos lighthouse at Alexandria might have looked. Other panels depict Nile scenes, animals, birds and fish, everyday rural life and Christian themes. The original site is to be found down a small track. There is also another church with a large mosaic still in place on the floor.

Pre-Islamic carvings at Sluntah

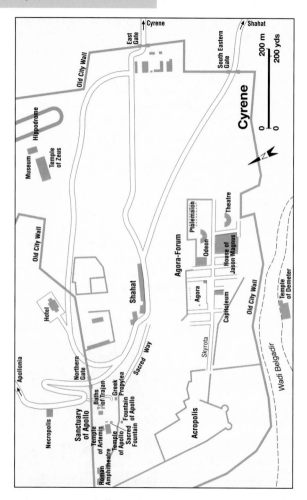

Cyrene

➤   About 20km (12 miles) from al-Bayda is **Sluntah** (open all the time, but ask for local guardian with key; free), the ancient necropolis of a primitive pre-Islamic funerary temple set around a natural cave. The walls are decorated with strange animal and human-like carvings in native Libyan styles which, significantly, show independence from Greco-Roman control. On the left is a long serpent moving into the cave, which is stacked with human heads. To the right is an altar with four wild boars or pigs on the offering table. The beliefs of the cult that worshipped here are unknown, but similar rituals are thought to have existed among Berbers and some desert tribes.

Cyrene

Tradition says that **Cyrene** (open daily 8am–5.30pm; admission fee) was founded in 631BC by King Battus and 200 inhabitants from the island of Thira (Santorini). Following years of drought and overcrowding, they consulted the oracle at Delphi, who told them to go to Libya.

At 600m (2,000ft) above sea level, Cyrene the most important city of Greek origin in North Africa, certainly bears a resemblance to Delphi as it drops down the hillside towards the sea on a series of ledges. Its early turbulent history seems to have been based on the cultivation and trade of silphium *(see box on page 74)*.

One of two lions presiding over Cyrene's Sacred Fountain

The site can be chronologically confusing, because reconstructions seen today were not all standing at the same time. Following Roman control there was widespread

The wealth of Cyrene and the Pentapolis cities seems to have been due mainly to a native plant called silphium. It was exported all over the Greek Empire, but would only grow in the special Jebel al-Akhdar conditions. The plant was noted for its medicinal properties, in particular as an early form of birth control. Sadly it was harvested to extinction.

destruction during the Jewish revolt in AD115, and some of the ruins remained for almost a century until Septimius Severus became a final benefactor until the city was further destroyed by the AD365 earthquake.

From the upper entrance amid the pine forests, the first site is the great rectangular enclosure with internal porticoes known as the **Ptolemaion**, probably used as a sports gymnasium. Its exact use is undetermined but it was converted into a **Roman Forum** and then military barracks in the 4th century. The small temple in the centre was possibly dedicated to Julius Caesar, but yielded a giant statue of Bacchus. Behind the forum is the small **Greek Theatre** or Odeon, badly damaged when it was converted for military use. Running behind this is a portico of alternating busts of Hermes and Heracles.

On the other side of the street is the **House of Jason Magus**, an important high priest of the Temple of Apollo, with the in-situ Four Seasons mosaic around a spiral design. A different type of marble inlay flooring (known as *opus sectile*) is found in the Triclinium, with wonderful open views across **Wadi Belgadir** to the Temple of Demeter and a recently excavated small theatre.

Back on the street is the House of the Labyrinth Mosaic, describing the famous tale of Ariadne, Theseus and the Minotaur. The street opens up into the **Agora** surrounded by civic buildings. The most unusual is the small semicircular building thought to be a sanctuary to Demeter and Kore (Persephone). In the centre are the roughly assembled blocks of a naval monument in the form of a trireme (a warship with three tiers of oars).

Buildings stretch further along this level towards the un-excavated Acropolis, but the pathway leads downwards to the right, past the Greek Baths, cave dwellings and the Sacred Way. Lower down are the four Doric columns of the **Greek Propylea**, and to the left is the **Fountain of Apollo**, the important water supply for the oldest part of the city. This is a delightful shady spot overlooking the Sanctuary of Apollo, often used by local families for picnics. Ahead of you, towards the sea are the Baths of Trajan to the right and the Temple of Apollo to the left. Between these two is a small reconstructed **Nymphaeum** or Sacred Fountain, with two lion statues. The **Temple of Apollo**, the most important

Cyrene's most important monument, the Temple of Apollo

monument, was rebuilt at least three times in antiquity, originally dating to the 6th century BC. The small temple on the right is dedicated to Artemis, the twin sister of Apollo and also dates from the earliest colony. A long altar stretches across the entrance of both temples.

About 150m (165yds) along the Sanctuary Terrace is the **Roman amphitheatre**, built on top of a smaller Greek theatre. The Roman audience would have completely surrounded the action, but the supported seating on the open northern side is now collapsed. Having inherited the site, the Romans were unable to construct suitable underground passageways and chambers for the wild animals, as the Greeks had built on solid rock. Covered entrances for the animals were built at ground level, which removed the lower tiers of Greek seating. Today there are wonderful views over the countryside from the top seats.

Before exiting the site, walk through the extensive **Baths of Trajan** begun in AD98, destroyed in the Jewish revolt of 115 and rebuilt by Hadrian a few years later. The rooms of differing temperature are laid out in logical fashion when entered from the original doorway near the cliff-face. Most of the statues inside the baths were buried by the collapsing roof in the AD365 earthquake and thus preserved until modern excavations. The Venus of Cyrene statue is now in Rome, but others such as the Three Graces and Alexander the Great (who never actually came here) are in the newly opened **Cyrene Museum**, beside the Temple of Zeus.

The gateway from the site will lead you past a local café towards the northern necropolis, a site used for entombing the dead from the earliest times. There are thousands of tombs cut into the rock, a large number of which have also acted as homes and shelters for hundreds of years. Carved stone sarcophagi, many with broken lids, are spread across the hillside.

Back at the top of the site, hidden within the pine forests is the impressive **Temple of Zeus**, a construction of enormous fluted-stone columns, and slightly larger than the Parthenon in Athens. Again, it dates to the earliest period around the 6th century BC, but was rebuilt several times. It was used to house a seated figure of Zeus, thought to have been around 12m (40ft) high. Some idea of its size can be judged by the tantalising fragments of huge marble fingernails on show in the site museum.

Behind this temple is a **Hippodrome**. It is still unexcavated, although it is possible to make out the curved southern end and some rows of seats through the undergrowth.

A welcome addition is the site **museum** (open Tues–Sun 8am–5.30pm; admission fee) opened in 2004, which houses some of the superb finds. The impressive central figure is a winged sphinx, standing on an Ionic capital from the Archaic period, similar to the Naxian sphinx in Delphi. It stood 6.2m (20ft) high, and was uncovered in 1963 from the necropolis that is now under the modern town. There are statues from the Baths of Trajan, earlier funerary statues, large carved sarcophagi and mosaics from the House of Jason Magus. An important carved block from 155BC shows the will of Ptolemy VII bequeathing

The Temple of Zeus

Apollonia's Eastern Basilica

Greek Cyrenaica to the Roman people, thus avoiding his assassination. One curious statue of Apollo can very clearly be seen as a re-working of an earlier statue to Aesclepios.

Apollonia

The port of **Apollonia** (open daily 8am–5.30pm; admission fee) was established in the 7th century BC just 20km (12 miles) from Cyrene. It was named after the patron god who originally brought the Greeks to Libya. Still surviving in Christian times, it was renamed Sozusa, corrupted by the Arabs into its present name of Susa.

Little is known about the site, except that it remained autonomous during Roman times and developed into a major city by the 6th century AD, from when most of these buildings date. The sea level was lower than it is today, but on calm days it is possible to see some of the walls and streets running into the sea. Originally there were eastern and western ports, but nowadays only some of the higher sections around the ports are high enough to break the waves, 300m (330yds) offshore. A shipwreck within the old port has been dated to the 4th century BC.

Immediately inside the site on the right is the **Western Basilica** dedicated to Rome, dating from the 4th century AD, built using blocks and columns from earlier collapsed buildings from the AD365 earthquake. A small baptistery is off to the side. Further along the coast is the **Central Basilica**, dedicated to St Mark, with an apse at each end. The white marble columns have exquisite carved crosses, and there are some sections of mosaics.

By the seashore are the Byzantine Baths, beside the earlier Roman version, which were reduced to being water-supply tanks. Inland are the ruins of a large **Palace**, which played an important role during the 6th century AD as the seat of government. Some of the rooms have been identified as a council chamber, audience hall, living quarters, private chapel and library. All of this was built above a giant water cistern to ensure that the whole complex could be self-contained.

The **Eastern Basilica** is the most impressive building with its many re-erected cippolino marble columns also from the 6th century. Some archaeologists suggest that its large size covers an earlier temple to Apollo. The remains of a font and sections of fine mosaics are scattered around, while others have been removed to the local museum. The path leads yet further past the Acropolis Hill, used as a quarry, and beyond the city walls are the remains of the **Greek Theatre**, now looking a little forlorn and almost slipping into the sea. A vast necropolis of the port is spread over the entire site, but much disturbed over the centuries.

Local women students from Cyrene

Returning along the coast and midway to the eastern church are the remains of huge grain stores hacked out of the solid rock, still with narrow necks, but now undermined and full of foaming sea water.

The site **museum** (open Tues–Sun 8am–5.30pm; admission fee) is on the edge of modern Susa town, but unfortunately has unpredictable opening times. It contains mosaics and reliefs from the site plus artefacts from Ras al-Hilal and al-Atrun.

The Eastern Coast

Along the coast, about 30km (19 miles) east of Apollonia, is an early Christian church of the 6th century AD, possibly dedicated to St Andrew, situated on a rocky headland called **Ras al-Hilal** (open all the time; free). It is robustly built, with the remains of a well, a cistern and a font, and even though the mosaics have been transported to Apollonia Museum, the spectacular location alone makes it worth a visit. The ancient name of this settlement appears to have been Naustatmos, and it might well have been the winter port for Cyrene rather than Apollonia. Recent Italian marine research offshore has identified over 30 cannons dating from the 17th century.

Located another 10km (6 miles) further east are two early Christian

View into the 6th-century church of Ras al-Hilal, east of Apollonia

churches of **al-Atrun**, formerly Athrun (open all the time; free), also beautifully situated on a clifftop overlooking the sea. An information plaque informs that the main western church can be dated from the nearby necropolis as 4th–6th century AD, and was possibly at one time a cathedral. There are some re-erected blue marble columns that were originally imported from the Sea of Marmara region of Turkey, as well as traces of a baptistery. The walls were faced with marble slabs adorned with carved crosses, sections of which lie pieced together on the ground. The site is beautiful in spring, when a carpet of flowers enhances the approach.

Located another 30km (19 miles) to the east is the modern city and harbour of **Derna** (Darnah), laid out along a thin coastal strip below impressive mountains. As the major centre of eastern Cyrenaica, Derna has several old and new mosques, a fruit-and-vegetable market and a covered *souq* selling gold and jewellery.

Inland, up a small wadi, is a waterfall known as Shallal Derna. This is an interesting place to break the journey towards Tobruk.

Tobruk

The name of **Tobruk** (Tubruq) conjures up images of dogged resistance and fierce attacks, as seen in so many World War II films. The harbour was coveted by both Allied and Axis troops for supplies, who fought over it during several drawn-out battles and sieges. Interestingly, as the probable site of Antipyrgos, it does not seem to have been of much importance in ancient times.

Lady Be Good

The remains of a B-24 bomber known as 'Lady Be Good' are stored in the small compound around Rommel's former HQ in Tobruk. The American plane set out to bomb Naples on 4 April 1943 but had to return to Benghazi because of engine trouble. Reduced visibility meant that it overflew the airfield and continued into the desert until it ran out of fuel. The crew parachuted out before the plane crashed. They tried to walk back to the coast, unaware that they were over 500km (300 miles) away. All died in the attempt, and it wasn't until 1958 that the wreckage was first spotted. The team leader of the expedition that brought the remains of the plane to Tobruk in 1994 was Dr Fadel Ali Mohamed, who can often be seen around the site at Cyrene.

The main reason to visit this area is to pay respects at the various **war cemeteries** (open all the time; free), of which there are two belonging to British and Commonwealth troops, maintained by the British War Graves Commission. The **Acroma Cemetery** is located 20km (12 miles) west of Tobruk overlooking the former battlefield that was nicknamed 'Knightsbridge' by the British troops. There are more than 3,500 burials in neat rows of graves with avenues of palm trees, all situated below a giant elevated cross. There are also shaded seated areas for quiet reflection and contemplation.

There are 2,500 graves in the Tobruk War Cemetery

Just 4km (2½ miles) south of the harbour is the **Tobruk War Cemetery**, fronted by the ship's bell of *HMS Liverpool*, with another 2,500 graves. The location is bright and airy, in total contrast to the **German Memorial**, which overlooks the harbour from on high, and is a brooding and solemn bastion to the 6,000 German troops who died. The **French Cemetery** is 6km (4½ miles) towards the airport, and contains the bodies of hundreds of soldiers killed mainly during the desert battle of Bir Hakim.

Inside the city are a few reminders, such as the headquarters of the German commander Marshal Rommel, surrounded by old field guns and armoured vehicles.

Trekking on the Saharan dunes in the vast Ubari Sand Sea

FEZZAN

Any tour down to the Fezzan region will undoubtedly pass through the main administration centre of **Sebha** (Sabha), almost 800km (500 miles) from Tripoli, either by direct flight to its airport or along the road south from Gharyan and Mizda. Sebha is also known as the 'first spark', as the initial moves of the revolution began here, where Colonel Gaddafi went to secondary school. The reverse of the 10LD notes shows a view of the people of Sebha, below the fort. The city itself is a logical starting point for a Sahara trip. It is here that you change into desert mode, with special guides, drivers and well-equipped four-wheel-drive vehicles. At a stretch you could stay in hotels or fixed camps and make day-trips to the sites, but it is more practical and adventurous to wild-camp amid the amazing desert scenery.

The eastward drive along **Wadi al-Hayat** (Valley of Life) is interesting as it passes through many settlements dating back to the times of the Garamantes people, a Libyan tribe mentioned by the Greek historian Herodotus as being powerful in this region. Possibly the ancestors of the modern Touareg, they acted as middlemen controlling the trade through the inhospitable desert from the central and southern Sahara, bringing gold, ivory, animals and slaves to the Mediterranean civilisations. They clashed with the Romans many times, but reached an uneasy peace, which lasted through the 2nd and 3rd centuries AD, the climax of their prosperity – at one time they even had their own section of the market at Leptis Magna.

Germa

Their capital was at **Germa**, 150km (95 miles) from Sebha, which has a fine though dusty museum (open Tues–Sun 8am–5.30pm; admission fee) on the main road, dealing with this period as well as the earlier rock art from the Acacus Mountains and carvings of the M'sak Settafet region. The original Garamantian settlement at Zinchecra was up in the mountains to the south, but later converted into a vast necropolis with tens of thousands of tombs, still being excavated.

About 1km (½ mile) north of the modern town, and surrounded by palm groves, is the ruined walled city of **Old Garama** (open daily 8am–5.30pm; admission fee), the oldest recorded truly Libyan city, dating from around the 1st century AD. It is home to the remains of a temple, public buildings, houses and a high kasbah at the far end. A series of mud-brick cities

Mud houses in Old Garama

on the same site has left a slightly confusing mass of destroyed and abandoned buildings from various periods up to the last century. The city was replaced by Murzuq and Zuwaylah (Zawīlah) further south as capital of the region, but continued to be an important trade centre and caravan town.

The Garamantes people conducted trade from sub-Saharan Africa to Leptis Magna. They brought slaves and wild animals for the amphitheatre games, as well as gold and semi-precious stones. Inscriptions at Leptis record gifts of elephants and tusks to the protecting gods of the city. Established even in Punic times, this trade developed in the 1st century AD through peaceful relations, and many goods travelled on to Rome and throughout the Empire.

To the west of the town along the main road to Ubari is a series of Garamantian cemeteries, housing small weathered pyramid tombs that measure approximately 3m (10ft) high. Of these, the principal site is al-Hatya.

Ubari

The area to the north is the vast **Ubari (Awbārī) Sand Sea** of continually changing dunes. It's a region that would normally be avoided entirely by humans, but the presence of small lakes in the centre of this arid expanse gives you the opportunity to see 'real' picturesque oases and the drivers a chance to show off their off-road expertise. The Ubari Lakes are an incredible sight and an amazing natural occurrence, which for centuries have sustained limited numbers of hardy settlers trying to survive here.

These people (and the lakes) are sometimes called Dawada – meaning 'worm eaters', a reference to the practice of scooping up, mashing and drying the tiny red shrimps that live in the lakes. As a lightweight dried food, full of protein, they were perfect for sustaining traders on long desert treks. There are a dozen or so lakes that have different characteristics – some are more saline, while others become mud and dry up, but all support a healthy fringe of palm trees, reeds and wildlife.

Four popular lakes to visit are **Umm al-Maa** and nearby **Mandara**, which sometimes dries up; also **Mavo** and **Gabroun**, which has a permanent campsite below a towering sand dune. This lake is said to be bottomless, which is hard to test, as everything (including swimmers) floats on the surface of the salty water; it does, however, seem to suit the tiny shrimps that still thrive there. Today the Ubari Lakes have been abandoned apart from a few Touareg souvenir sellers from Niger who rely on the tourists visiting from Germa. Camping in this area is a real Saharan experience, with sharp ridges of softer dunes sculpted by the wind swirling in every direction.

Umm al-Maa, one of the Ubari Lakes

Tadrart-Acacus Mountains

Back on the road past al-Awinat (al-Uwaynāt), heading further west towards the Algerian border is the pleasant Touareg town of **Ghat**, the bustling centre for all visits into the Acacus Mountains and the wadis containing ancient rock art. If you are not visiting Ghadames then a walk into the old city is highly recommended; even though it measures only 400m x 200m (440yds x 220yds), Ghat's old city offers a wonderful atmosphere of security, trade and desert survival. Note the tamarisk, acacia and palm wood used as roof beams above the covered streets. A five-minute walk up to the fort provides stunning views over the old and new towns, towards the Tassili n'Ajjer plateau in Algeria to the west and the Acacus Mountains to the east, an extension of the Tadrart region of Algeria.

Examples of rock art in the Tadrart-Acacus Mountains

The oasis owes its importance to its strategic position, initially as a Garamantian outpost. Even a century ago it was the only caravan route open from Niger to Tripolitania, as Touareg raids and political unrest had closed all other routes. The predominance of French speakers in Ghat reflects the continued strong links with Algeria and French Africa to the south and west.

On a typical desert safari, the convoy of suitably equipped vehicles passes out of Ghat and soon enters the Tadrart-Acacus range, which is now a National Park with a couple of checkpoints. There are no set routes, timings or itineraries, and all depends on what agreement you have with your guide and drivers, but generally three or four days are the minimum to get to the main **rock art** sites of pictographs and pictograms. Most tours involve driving south to skirt round the southern tip of the Acacus and working back north along the other side, visiting the sites of rock art and natural formations en route, until meeting the main road again somewhere near al-Awinat.

There are no useful maps, with locations being further complicated by Touareg names of the wadis, and art sites having many variations in local Arabic. The two main routes

Four Ages of Rock Art

Most of the rock art found in the Acacus region of the Sahara dates from around 4000BC, when the climate was cooler and wetter than it is today. Archaeologists studying these paintings and carvings argue about the dates, but generally have classified them into four distinct periods.

The first period (8000–5000BC) is typified by the giant 'round head' human figures with associated symbols and shapes. The second period (5000–2000BC) has a more naturalistic style of both paintings and carvings, featuring wild animals such as elephant, giraffe, crocodiles, ostrich and antelopes. Domestic cattle and horses also start to appear. The third period (2000BC–AD500) occurs when the climate changes and with it the range of animals. Cattle are replaced by camels, and there are figures that could be the mysterious Garamantians in chariots. The fourth period (after AD500) sees the use of an early script, possibly by the Garamantians, who could be the ancestors of the Touareg people.

are along **Wadi Tashwinat** (Tashween or Tashwent) and **Wadi Anchil** (Anshal).

There are thousands of sites of rock art, some of which you may even find on your own wanderings, but the guides will take you to a dozen or so of the best and most prolific that cover the main periods and styles *(see box on page 89)*. Some of the realistically accurate animals being chased by hunters are frozen in mid-action, while other scenes are more like a record of pastoral harmony between man and domesticated cattle.

Little is known about the people who made the paintings or why they chose certain sites, but they do seem to be places of significance as paintings of many periods often overlap each other, leaving huge areas of 'blank canvas' near by completely untouched. Generally speaking, the paintings are protected inside naturally eroded shelters,

A rock arch frames the desert and the Tadrart-Acacus Mountains

whereas the few carvings in the Acacus are in the open on exposed slabs. One of the main conclusions to be drawn from this is that the Sahara must have had a much wetter climate and sufficient vegetation to support the range of animals painted and carved on the rocks 4,000 years ago.

The security policeman with your group will be watchful of your actions, following a history of damage to the unique pieces of art. Some has been caused

The Touareg have controlled the desert trade for centuries

by ignorance, like the wetting of the figures to highlight the colours for photographs or the use of bright lights and flash photography. But there have also been cases of wilful damage, from the treatment and peeling of colours off painted figures, to the complete hacking out of sections of rock wall.

Access to the sites by four-wheel-drive is generally very good, with nothing more needed than a scramble up some rocks or a short slog up a sand dune. Liaise with the guide and drivers and try to arrange some time for a walk of an hour or two to soak up the vastness, splendour and silence of the wadis, without getting into any danger. Even without the ancient art, the Acacus region would be worth investigating for its breathtaking landscape of towering cliffs, sweeping dunes and massive eroded rock sculptures. The spectacular natural **rock arch** at the end of Wadi Anchil is on every itinerary, with groups camping in the isolated wadis near by.

There are several tracks leading back to the main road to Sebha, but for the really adventurous there is the northeast route across bleak landscapes into the area of the **M'sak Settafet**, a rock-strewn wilderness running roughly parallel to the main road. The main interest here is in **Wadi Matkhandoush** and the vast number of rock carvings, featuring wild animals now associated with East African safaris – elephants, hippos, crocodiles, large cats and giraffes. As with the Acacus art, little is known about the people who carved these images, which could go back over 4,000 years. There are photographs and copies of the main pieces in the museum at Germa.

The Remote South and East
The **Tibesti Massif** is located midway along the border with Chad, and until recently was out of bounds to tourist groups. Those that have been claim it to be the most spectacular

There are still vast areas of the Libyan Sahara to be explored

scenery anywhere in the Sahara, but there are concerns about security and safety. Libya and Chad engaged in some fierce fighting along this border in the 1980s over the disputed mineral-rich Ouzo Strip, and there are still many routes and tracks that have not been checked or cleared of landmines.

Fennec foxes roam the desert

A long way north of the Tibesti is a range of dramatic extinct volcanoes, some filled with water, around Waw al-Namoos. If you do get permission to organise a full-scale expedition to the Tibesti, Tripoli to Sebha is only halfway.

Only 200km (125 miles) to the east of Sebha is a surreal area known as the **al-Haruj al-Aswad** (Black Volcanic Plateau), a chain of ancient peaks surrounded by the blackened exposed debris of earlier volcanic eruptions.

Given the huge size of Libya, current tourism only scratches the surface of the natural wonders of the Saharan landscape and there are vast areas still be to be explored. As oil and water projects continue to venture into the desert, this at least gives some promising tracks for further exploration – especially down in the remote southeast of al-Khalij around the al-Kufrah oasis, a remote base used by the Long Range Desert Group (forerunners of the SAS) for their attacks behind enemy lines on German bases during World War II.

Further south, close to the border with Sudan, are the Jebel Arknu and Jebel al-Uweinat mountains, which also contain ancient rock art, and were the setting for the real-life drama about Laszlo Almasy, fictionalised in the book and film *The English Patient*.

WHAT TO DO

As tourism is in its infancy in Libya, there are as yet few diversions for visitors beyond historical and cultural attractions. However, the opportunities for adventure sports are tremendous. Given the country's limited infrastructure, it is often a case of bringing your own equipment and getting on with it, but you might be able to track down like-minded people inside Libya. The majority of Libyans are spectators of team sports such as football, basketball and volleyball, rather than participants.

OUTDOOR PURSUITS

If you engage in any adventure activity, make sure that you are well prepared, qualified and insured to do it, and expect to be self-sufficient. Any accidents could have serious consequences, as medical facilities are limited. Do not forget that this all has to be done under the guidance of a tour agency, probably with a rep appointed to go with you, or at least account for you at the start and finish of each day.

Watersports

Probably the most developed activity, although still in its infancy, is scuba-diving, with several dive shops on the Medina seafront in Tripoli and in Benghazi. The best sites are away from the cities, especially around al-Khoms and Misrata to the east and Janzour to the west: there is a dive centre at the Janzour Beach Resort *(see page 136)*. It is mostly done by a few local professional divers rather than as a sport, but at least there is the PADI Arebi Diving Centre in Tripoli run by Mohammed Arebi, mobile tel: +218 (91) 320 1089; also Mohandes Khalid,

Handmade gold and silver jewellery is good value in the *souqs*

Inspecting rock art on a high ledge in the Tadrart-Acacus Mountains

mobile tel: +218 (91) 212 3899. In Benghazi there is the Ammar dive shop in the city centre, mobile tel: +218 (92) 510 6130. Most speak no English, so it's much more convenient to get one of the tour agencies to contact them and ask them to put a package together. As a foreigner you would need permission to dive, and the tourist authorities are nervous about people scuba-diving on any ancient ruins, such as off Apollonia, but you should be permitted to snorkel in those areas. Snorkelling and other watersports such as swimming, sailing, windsurfing, jet skiing and water skiing are generally only available (if at all) at beach resorts away from the city centre.

Trekking

The potential for trekking is endless, with many spectacular walking areas often not far from main cities such as the Jebel Nafusa near Tripoli and the Green Mountains inland from Benghazi. No detailed maps exist, so it is very much down to practicalities such as location of overnight accommodation or camping, or parking to enable a circular walk to be completed. One or two adventure-tour operators manage half- or full-day treks during their cultural itineraries.

Around the village of Jadu in Jebel Nafusa is the walk from town, westwards down the gorge to Ain Zaga (the Blue-Eyed Spring), a natural oasis pool at the foot of a cliff, and the walk along the edge of the escarpment to the spectacular abandoned village of Tormeisa. The climb from Qasr al-Haj to Tormeisa would be tough but rewarding.

In the Green Mountains of Cyrenaica, there are wonderful treks around Wadi al-Kuf near al-Bayda, where sections of the old Italian mountain road can be walked.

Desert treks are offered as organised tours by some operators and agencies in the Acacus Mountains. They are popular with French and Italian groups as a way to visit the rock-art sites, and can be supported by camel or four-wheel-drive. Camel treks cover greater distances and especially in the Ubari Lakes dunes area give a real taste of the trans-Saharan trade routes, camping out at night beneath the stars.

Desert Driving

One activity that is gaining popularity is four-wheel-drive desert driving, again especially with the French and Italians, who bring their own well-equipped vehicles via Tunisia. These can be amazing adventures, taking

Visiting one of the old bath houses known as *hammams* is an interesting excursion at the end of a scorching day, and a chance to meet the locals. Language is seldom a barrier at these unofficial same-sex social events, and it is a particularly good opportunity for women to see the lives of local women. There are one or two *hammams* in the Tripoli Medina, with different opening days and times for men and women.

Driving in the desert needs careful preparation and local knowledge

you to little-known areas such as the volcanic lakes of Waw al-Namoos, but they need to be well organised, with paperwork and permissions arranged. Libya is not the place suddenly to change your itinerary and decide to go somewhere else. It can also be expensive, as you will probably need to hire another four-wheel-drive for your national guide, security policeman and local Bedouin guide.

Specialist four-wheel-drive tour companies based in the Fezzan are subcontracted to operate all the desert trips for the Tripoli-based tour agencies, and they might be persuaded to let you learn and improve off-road skills using their vehicles. Try Ahmed al-Ajely at Om el-Ramil Tours in Sebha, tel: +218 (71) 634569, email: <omelramil4@yahoo. com>, or reach him through Wings Tours in Tripoli. Also try the local company Alawy Tours *(see Guides and Tours, page 120)*.

Variations on this are the group tours offered by Italian companies, where you join a team of off-road motorcyclists in the Acacus/Ghat region. Riding specially prepared trail bikes brought from Italy, you are instructed and led by desert experts (some from the famous Paris–Dakar rally). But beware, as there are always accidents requiring hospitalisation along the 650km (400 miles). Try <www.airzoone.com>.

Bikes and Horses

Mountain biking – something new to Libya – offers endless possibilities, as many roads in the country are still dirt tracks, especially in the mountain areas. As with trekking, you will need to be self-sufficient and have a good sense of direction (or a compass).

There is a great tradition of horsemanship in Libya, especially amongst the desert tribes. Horse riding, including jumping, racing and competitions, is enjoyed by a limited number of Libyans, mainly along the Tripolitanian coast. There are a number of small equestrian centres here, which generally belong to families. As yet there are no organised horse treks or rides for visitors, as horses are expensive to own and keep. For further information, try the Adiat Horse Club in Tripoli, tel: (021) 486 4330.

Shooting

If you are a marksman then try the Libyan Shooting and Archery Federation (in Tripoli), which looks after the sport in Libya. It organises tournaments including darts and skeet, and is a member of the ISSF, FITA, FATA and ASF, tel: (021) 478 0481-6, fax: (021) 478 0510. A more exotic form of hunting is done by visitors from Gulf countries who hunt with falcons, especially in the remote al-Haruj al-Aswad lava field region.

Less harmful is bird watching, and there are many migrants regularly flying between Europe and Africa in addition to a wide range of resident birds.

SHOPPING

Many domestic goods are imported, as locals have abandoned their traditional crafts, so finding true Libyan goods can be hit and miss. Even the beautiful displays of pots and bowls around the country's pottery centre of Gharyan contain items from Tunisia, but they still make good souvenirs. Haggling over prices is not common in Libya, but you can sometimes negotiate a better deal by buying several items at once. Quality clothing can be expensive, especially the heavy coats worn by both men and women in the winter, but a long flowing *galabiya* is a useful and practical item of clothing, especially if you are heading out into the desert. There are also many styles and colours of headgear to complete the Libyan look, including the *chechia* black felt cap.

Carpets and rugs for sale in the Tripoli Medina

Gold, silver and jewellery shops are always busy inside the Medina in Tripoli and along Souq al-Jareed in Benghazi, with attractive prices for visitors. Leather goods such as bags and jackets can be found just inside the Tripoli Medina gateway to the left, together with a range of bright carpets, rugs and sheepskins.

For new art, try the Ghadames Art Gallery at 50 1 September Street in Tripoli, tel: (021) 333 6666. It

In the Fezzan, many of the souvenir sellers are from Niger, offering Touareg crosses from different regions, but these are not normally made from silver as they claim. Their glittering spreads of bracelets, bead necklaces, bangles, camel leather tassels, basketware, purses, bags, knives and swords in the barren sands of Ubari add a photogenic splash of colour.

has been run for 25 years by Mustafa Gaim and his family, and is packed with hundreds of original oils, pastels, watercolours and prints, representing many local artists. There is also an album of old 1920–60s photographs, from which you can order copies. Just down the street is the useful Dar Fergiani bookshop, with a good selection of reprints of old desert adventures and early travel writing.

There are curio shops off Green Square with piles of dusty oddments in the streets that are enjoyable to rummage through. Metalwork plates and trays come in all sizes, some with an engraved profile of the Colonel himself.

For sale in the shops of small towns such as Ghat, Germa and al-Awinat are the Touareg head cloths in bright colours, very useful for keeping sun and sand at bay.

One way to find more esoteric items is to visit one of the weekly markets in the rural areas. These are great social occasions for the villagers but also opportunities to buy local products, in most cases direct from the craftsmen. Check out

Colourful Gharyan pots

the rugs and carpets (especially in Berber regions), pottery and palm-frond mats and baskets, as well as natural produce such as local honey and fruit juice.

Locally produced CDs and cassettes are good value. A unique gift would be a sheet of postage stamps making a propaganda statement, for example about the American bombing of Tripoli.

ENTERTAINMENT

Public entertainment in Libya is almost non-existent, as everything revolves around family life in the home. Without any local contacts, the choices for an evening out are extremely limited, and in some places could be down to seeing a film in Arabic at a cinema or strolling to the nearest teahouse. Join the local men for a game of dominoes, backgammon or smoke a *nargila* 'hubble-bubble' pipe, a traditional Arabic smoke with a variety of tobacco of different flavours like apple, mint, grape or rose petals. In Tripoli try the ramshackle floating teahouse called the Lebda, a converted boat in the harbour just off the Red Castle. If you do have local connections then this might stretch to a family celebration or wedding festivity that can last several days. Some places only come alive in the evenings, so try the fish market of Busitta *(see Eating Out)*.

If you try desert camping, some of the most memorable evenings will be spent sitting around the campfire listening to the guides, drivers and cooks singing and playing local instruments. Also check out the evening camel market in Sebha.

You might have planned your visit to coincide with special events such as the Ghadames Festival in November or the one at Kabaw in April, when there is music and dance in the evenings. You might be lucky and come across a performance at one of the theatres of Sabratha or Leptis. In Ghadames at any time of the year you could extend your sunset visit to the dunes by asking for an evening barbecue to be organised in addition to the traditional tea making and *tajeelah* sand-baked bread. On some evenings there is live music and singing at the Corinthia Hotel in Tripoli, and even versions of western Libyan music at the Rock in the lively suburb of Gargaresh.

As in other North African countries, football is followed with great passion. Ask if there is a game taking place at the stadiums of Benghazi or Tripoli. All towns and cities have pool and billiard halls, where you can take on the locals.

Festivals

Libya observes all the main Muslim festivals, the dates of which change each year. **Eid al-Fitr** and **Eid al-Adha** may last anything from two to 10 days depending on the region, and are great times for celebration. Check exact dates for all festivals with tour operators.

April A festival celebrating Berber traditions is held at Kabaw in the Nafusa Mountains.

September The main secular holiday is Revolution Day on 1 September, marked with a week of public parades, rallies and events including folk troupes, horsemen and music groups.

October Date-harvest festivals are held in various parts of the country.

November The annual Ghadames International Festival is when the Old City comes briefly back to life for three days. Houses open up for Touareg folkloric music, dance and wedding celebrations.

December The colourful Ghat Festival takes place at the end of December, famous for its music, dancing and Touareg camel races.

EATING OUT

The Libyans do not have a great tradition of eating out at restaurants, and, though this is slowly changing, there is certainly a lack of choice even in the major cities. Until recently, foreigners were catered for by expensive and indifferent meals in the large government hotels, but the recent dramatic rise in visitor numbers has meant that there is now a better choice for eating out. But in towns with one good tourist hotel, such as Zliten, Ghadames or Sebha, there is not enough trade to sustain a private restaurant that's too expensive for local pockets. Often the only alternative to eating at the hotel restaurant will be the grilled chicken parlours and pizzerias popular with younger Libyans. Group hotels serve Western set menus or have international buffets, which vary from excellent to bland.

Traditional food prepared over an open fire in the desert

Most city restaurants will offer similar menus; the only difference is whether they specialise in fish or some other local dish, such as *jarra*. Some dishes are never made outside the private home, and unless you are invited to a house, your best chance could be while camping in the desert, with meals prepared by a local cook.

For a different experience, try the evening fish market of Busitta, also known as al-Hofra ('the Hole') close to the Palm Beach on Fatah Road, west along the coast from Tripoli. Here you can buy fresh fish direct from the fishermen and then have it cleaned, gutted and cooked to your liking in front of you.

If you are lucky enough to be invited to a Libyan house for a meal, guests are served first. The women of the family will place platters of food in the middle of the table and people help themselves. Traditionally, people eat with the fingers of the right hand (the left hand is considered unclean and is not used).

As in everyday life, Muslim laws determine aspects of Libyan diet. Alcohol, pork and any food containing pork fat are forbidden, and all meat must be halal.

WHAT TO EAT

With all the historical influences, it is not surprising that Libyan cuisine is an eclectic mix of Mediterranean food incorporating Turkish, Greek, French, Italian and North African styles. Lamb, beef, chicken, beans, nuts, dried fruit, figs and unleavened bread are the main ingredients of Libyan meals, which can be spiced up with *harissa*, a red-hot chilli paste.

Breakfast is usually a light continental meal of tea or coffee with bread and jam, but if you have a chance, try the delicious vegetarian *fool madammas* (fava bean stew), a hot substantial Egyptian dish eaten in the morning. The main meal of the day is served between 1 and 3pm, as businesses and schools close to allow families to get together. If the day is hot, the main meal can be taken in the cool of the evening, when most socialising takes place. Plan to eat by 8.30pm, as establishments close early if trade is slack.

Starters

Sharba Libya (Libyan soup) is one of the truly characteristic dishes, a delicious thick broth made from lamb, onion, tomato, red pepper and *hararat* (Libyan spices) with a refreshing dash of mint, coriander and lemongrass. *Shakshooka*, with or without meat, is a tasty mixture of onions, tomatoes, chilli peppers and egg served in small dishes. *Sharbat hoot* (fish soup) is good and spicy, as are *koftat hoot* (fish cakes).

Salads of various types are sometimes served alongside soup with different kinds of bread and well-known dips such as hummus, a savoury mixture of puréed chickpeas, lemon, sesame tahini, oil and spices.

Main Courses

Lamb is the most popular meat, and can be cooked in many different ways, though beef and chicken are becoming increasingly common. The Libyan *tagine* is different from the Moroccan version: here it is spicy lamb with a rich tomato sauce. As in the rest of North Africa, couscous (granular semolina) is popular, especially in western Libya, served with meat, potatoes, vegetables and dried fruits. There are many versions, including *couscous bil bosla*, with spicy lamb or beef, beans, potatoes, onions, tomatoes, chillis and peppers; *cous-cous bil ghiddeed*, with dried

> Some restaurants can offer the local speciality *jarra*, a substantial dish of meat or fish prepared and cooked inside a jar. Due to the preparation and cooking time, it should be ordered at least three hours before.

meat and green beans; and the fish dish *couscous bil hoot*. Rice dishes are more common in the east, and come in many varieties, such as *ruzz ja'ari*, a highly seasoned aromatic rice to be served with lamb and tomato; and *ruzz bil khaloot*, rice cooked with chopped liver, almonds and other nuts. Also popular in Cyrenaica is *rishda*, a dish of handmade macaroni topped with lamb or beef, lentils, fenugreek, beans, chickpeas, garlic and tomato.

Vegetarians are not particularly well catered for, but there will always be salads and eggs on offer. The base

The ubiquitous grilled chicken

of most meat dishes is couscous, pasta or rice, and these can be taken with just vegetables, as in *couscous bil khodra*. If you can find them, there are local non-meat dishes including *lubya bil selk*, a dish of white beans with spinach. *Tabahij* is usually a side dish made with courgette, potato, aubergine, onion and tomato, but is filling enough as a main course.

Despite almost 1,800km (1,100 miles) of coastline, the amount of fish and seafood caught is negligible, and until recently fish was not a major feature in Libyan diets. However, this is changing, and several restaurants in Tripoli are keen to promote themselves as fish specialists, with red snapper and sea bass topping the list. Seafood cocktails and squid are generally very good. *Haraymi* is a fish marinated in cumin and lemon, then spicily cooked in a delicious onion, tomato, garlic and parsley sauce.

Desserts

Year-round, quality locally grown fruit includes grapes, apricots, peaches, nectarines, fresh dates and citrus fruits. Depending on the size of the restaurant you might be offered any one of the following: *laseeda*, a sticky flour dish of honey and sugar; *magrood*, a long date roll cut into small pieces, glazed in boiling syrup and decorated with sesame seeds; *basboosah*, a rich syrup-filled cake cut into diamond-shaped pieces that you will see laid out in patisseries; and *mhalbiya*, a rice pudding with cinnamon and nuts, and eaten cold.

Tomatoes feature prominently in the Libyan diet

Snacks

The universal *shawarma* (sliced meat with tomatoes and salad inside pitta bread) is fast food eaten on the move. New patisseries are opening in large towns with a range of sweet pastries such as *magrood* and *basboosah*, great with a coffee. *Ka'k* are savoury twirls of dough of many varities. *Bureks* will be familiar to many travellers as the hand-sized pastry packets filled with spinach, meat, cheese, potato or egg.

Drinks

With a complete ban on alcohol, there is more emphasis on juices, soft drinks and hot beverages. For a change try the refreshing tart tamarind. Non-alcoholic beers are widely available, and some of the better-known brands are surprisingly good.

Service with a smile

When it comes to coffee, the choice is limited to *qahwa*, the thick black Arab (Turkish) coffee, and instant, which is usually simply referred to as Nescafé. There are some impressive Italian coffee machines, but you are unlikely to get a really good cappuccino.

Ramadan

In Libya all restaurants close through the day to observe the month of fasting. Non-Muslims are not expected to fast, but they are expected to be discreet about when and where they eat and drink. Special foods are prepared during Ramadan for the evenings, as well as for weddings and the Eid religious feasts.

To Help You Order

bread	**khubza**	without meat	**bidoon laham**
butter	**zibda**	coffee	**qahwa**
chicken	**djaij**	with milk	**bil haleeb**
eggs	**bayd, dahi**	without sugar	**bidoon sukar**
fish	**hoot, samak**	glass of tea	**tasat shay**
rice	**ruzz**	the bill,	**al hessab**
soup	**sharba**	please	**min fadlak**

HANDY TRAVEL TIPS

An A–Z Summary of Practical Information

A

ACCOMMODATION (see also CAMPING, YOUTH HOSTELS and
RECOMMENDED HOTELS)

As Libya expands its tourist industry, the accommodation available is
lagging behind demand, especially over the busy Christmas and Easter
periods. For many years, the larger 'international' hotels catered for business visitors and charged accordingly. A tourist class of accommodation,
including beach complexes, is slowly developing, but there is a lack of
good-quality mid-range hotels even in the large cities or close to the main
tourist sites. Outside the cities, one reason that many tour itineraries look
so similar is that groups often stay in the only suitable hotel.

Beach resorts around Tripoli are popular summer getaways for
Libyans and get fully booked up, but are not normally geared to the
demands of international tourism. The Ministry of Tourism is plan-
ning five new coastal tourist resorts for the future.

For desert safari trips around the Fezzan there are fixed tourist
camps which are often better than relying on overstretched hotel
options *(see Camping)*.

Most top hotels are extremely security-conscious, and will make
you pass through an airport-style metal detector upon entry. Your
accommodation should be booked by your agency at the time of
visa application. The best advice is to book ahead as far as possible, be flexible and not raise your expectations.

Do you have a …	**Hal fee ghurfa …**
single/double room?	**fardiya/zawjiya?**
How much per night?	**Bekam a layla?**

AIRPORTS

Since the dropping of sanctions, many routes have been re-established,
and there are now direct flights from many European cities. Tripoli

International Airport is located at Ben Ghashir, 25km (15 miles) south of the city. There are currency exchanges, a post office, restaurant and the usual airport shops. Porters are available to help with luggage. A bus service runs to the city centre, but the best option is to hire a taxi and agree the fare in advance (approximately 30LD). From the city out to the airport, a taxi is about 20LD.

When departing from Tripoli, allow plenty of time for check-in, after which you can use the departures coffee shop, internet and post office (using LD), or the Duty Free (using US dollars or euros). There is no departure tax.

Benghazi Benina International Airport is 18km (11 miles) from the city centre.

Some internal flights to and from Tripoli (such as with Buraq Air) may use the smaller Maatiqa airport (one money-exchange office), 4km (2½ miles) east of Tripoli city centre. For security reasons you may need to identify your baggage, laid out on the tarmac, immediately before boarding the plane.

B

BICYCLE HIRE (RENTAL)

Cycling is not a popular pastime in Libya. Hiring (or borrowing) a bicycle is more likely to be through a personal contact or a friendly bike shop in a major town, but you could be risking your life in the traffic with no helmets available. The only place that it would seem worthwhile and safe to explore by bike would be in laid-back Ghadames. Other than that you would need to bring your own, with sufficient spares.

BUDGETING FOR YOUR TRIP

Flights direct to Libya are expensive when compared to neighbouring destinations. The following prices in LD will give you a rough idea of how much you will spend inside the country, even though a lot of these costs will probably already be included in the tour costs by the tour agency.

Visa on arrival: US$25.

Airport transfer: from Tripoli International Airport to Green Square 30LD.

Car hire: from 70LD per day.

Guides: official guides from 50LD per half-day, 90 LD full day.

Hotels: double room with bath/shower per night: one-star 50LD, two-star 50–100LD, three-star 100–150LD, four-star 150–300LD, five-star from 300LD.

Internal flights: usually below 50LD one-way.

Internet cafés: 1LD per hour

Meals and drinks: breakfasts are normally included in room rates. Set menu or buffet lunch/dinner in two/three-star hotel or site restaurant 15–20LD, in four-star hotel 30–40LD. Evening meal in city restaurant 25–50LD. Soft drink/coffee in café 1LD.

Shared taxis: 5LD per 100 km.

Sightseeing: admission to museum/archaeological site 3LD plus camera ticket 5LD and video ticket 10LD.

Taxis: 5km (3-mile) trip across Tripoli 10LD.

C

CAMPING

There are few organised campsites, but there seems little problem camping almost anywhere within reason. Try to camp away from urban areas, seek the permission of the landowner and inform the local police. Camping on the beach is perhaps ideal, but not recommended within sight of military or industrial areas. In the Fezzan, most groups are obliged to camp, either in fixed camps or out in the open (wild-camping). Fixed camps in Sebha, al-Awinat, Germa, Ubari and Ghat offer double tents or small local-style huts, with toilets, shower blocks and on-site restaurant.

CAR HIRE (RENTAL) (see also Driving)

Although several car-hire companies offer vehicles in the bigger hotels, there are several important points worth mentioning. Your Arabic should be good enough to argue with traffic police at check-points and to read road signs. All foreign visitors should be accompanied by a security/tourist policeman and a tour-agency representative. If you do hire a car you will need your national licence, international driving permit, and photocopies of your passport and visa. Expect to pay upwards of US$50 per day. Most drivers and vehicles in Libya are uninsured, another important consideration.

I want to hire a car…	**Ureed astajer siyara…**
now/tomorrow	**towa/bukra**
day/week	**yom/isboa**
international driving permit	**tasreah kiyadah dowli**
local driving licence	**rukhsat kiyadah**

CLIMATE

The main influence on the climate along the developed northern coast is the cooling Mediterranean Sea. This gives mild winters and warm summers, with a pleasant range of mean temperatures throughout the year between 8°C and 30°C (46–86°F), although it can climb to over 35°C (95°F) in summer. It can become unpleasant in the west during the spring, when the northerly *gebli* wind blows dust and sand from the Sahara, raising the humidity. Cyrenaica tends to be cooler because of its altitude, with the very occasional snow flurry in winter, when the rest of the archaeological sites can be caught in downpours under leaden skies. Rainfall averages 380mm (15in) per year.

Most of the country (90 percent) is arid desert or semi-desert, where the main influence is the Sahara, causing frequent periods of drought. Daily autumn, winter and spring temperatures in the desert can rise to 25°C (77°F), but overnight it can drop to below freezing, especially with wind-chill. In the summer it can reach 50°C (122°F). In 1922, Libya recorded the world-record highest temperature, at al-Azizia, just south of Tripoli, when it reached 58°C (136°F).

CLOTHING

Lightweight cotton and linen clothing is ideal during the day, through the summer months in the north and year-round in the desert. Arms and legs should be covered for sun protection, local respect and when visiting religious sites. Take a sunhat, high-factor suncream and sunglasses. Evenings can be cold, especially at altitude or in the desert in winter, when warm clothing is needed. Throughout the winter months there is always the chance of rain, so a jacket is handy.

Swimwear is only acceptable on the beaches and around hotel pools. Topless bathing is not allowed anywhere. Comfortable walking shoes are best for the desert and the extensive archaeological sites. Local women are usually well covered, sometimes with the *hijab* black head cover and *jilbab* full-length coat.

CRIME AND SAFETY

Libya is a very safe country to travel in, with a great deal of security and stability. Street crime is almost unheard of. However, there are always opportunists, especially in crowded areas such as bus stations and busy *souqs*. Most Libyans are friendly, curious and hospitable to foreigners, but be wary of the recent influx of sub-Saharan Africans who trade on the streets and hang around the shared taxi ranks, especially at night. All tour groups are accompanied by a dedicated security/tourist policeman whose duty is to oversee the safety of the group, and will often pre-empt any situations they consider to be unsafe.

I have lost my passport…	**Reyaht al jawaz…**
wallet	**disdan**
handbag	**shuntah**

CUSTOMS AND ENTRY REQUIREMENTS (see also EMBASSIES AND CONSULATES and GUIDES AND TOURS)

In 2005 regulations changed to allow the issuing of visas at your arrival airport or border crossing. Tourist visas for single and group tourists for Libya are currently only possible as part of an organised tour. Although this may change, independent travel in Libya is not yet permitted. Tourist and business visas are required by visitors of all nationalities except those of other Arab countries. Your passport must be valid for a minimum of six months and must not contain any stamps or other indication that you have visited Israel. American citizens are welcomed by the Libyan authority.

The process for getting a visa starts with contacting a Libyan tour agency or an international tour operator at least six weeks before your planned departure. You require an invitation from your incoming agent, who then needs details of your passport and personal information, date of arrival and departure etc, depending on current regulations. These are then translated into Arabic by your tour agency, who will have the paperwork at immigration for your arrival. Despite the new regulations, some airlines still seem unsure about letting passengers on flights without a visa stamped in the passport, so be sure to check before leaving.

Up-to-date information can be obtained from your tour operator, tour agency or visa specialist, such as Travcour <www.travcour.com> and TDS <www.traveldocs.com>.

Inside Libya, hotels require you to leave your passport in a secure reception area for the duration of your stay, but you will need it to change money at a bank or exchange. You must register your passport with the police authorities within seven days. It is strictly forbidden to bring any alcohol, prohibited drugs or pork products into the country.

(I have) nothing forbidden	**mafeesh mamnu'at**

D

DRIVING (see also CAR HIRE/RENTAL)

If you intend to drive a car you will need your national licence, international driving permit, and photocopies of your passport and visa. Most visitors only drive if they are bringing in their own vehicle, as do many four-wheel-drive enthusiasts from Europe via Tunisia.

In Libya you need to travel with a guide (around US$50 in your vehicle – at least twice that in their own car).

E

ELECTRICITY

Libya uses 220–240v/50Hz current, so most European appliances will be fine. The supply is good and reliable. US appliances on 110v need a transformer. Sockets are mainly standard Continental European round two-pin plugs, but there are some square three-pins.

EMBASSIES AND CONSULATES (see also GUIDES AND TOURS and CUSTOMS AND ENTRY REQUIREMENTS)

British Embassy: Burj al-Fateh, 24th Floor, Tower 2, Tripoli; tel: consular (021) 340 3644/5; commercial (021) 335 1084/5/6; <www.britain-in-libya.org>.

US Embassy: The consular representative's office is located in the Belgian Embassy at Dhat al-Imad, 5th Floor, Tower 4, Tripoli; tel: (021) 333 3771 or 335 0115; fax: (021) 335 0118; email: <tripoli@diplo bel.org>. There are limited services available for US citizens.

US Liaison Office: Temporarily located at the Corinthia Bab Africa Hotel, Souk al-Thulatha, Al-Gadim, Tripoli; tel: (021) 335 1848; fax: (021) 335 1847.

Canadian Embassy: Burj al-Fateh, 7th Floor, Tower 1, Tripoli; tel: (021) 335 1633; fax: (021) 335 1630; email <trpli@dfait-maeci.gc.ca>.

Australia: The embassy in Cairo handles Libyan affairs; tel: +202 575 0444. Consular assistance in Libya is given by the British Embassy.
South Africa: The embassy in Tunisia also handles Libyan affairs; email: <sa@emb-safrica.intl.tn>.

For information about visas (and limited tourist information), try:
UK: The Libyan People's Bureau, 61–2 Ennismore Gardens, London SW7 1NH; tel: 020 7589 6109/20.
US: The Libyan Liaison Office, 2600 Virginia Avenue NW, Suite 705, Washington DC 20037; tel: 202-944-9601; fax: 202-944-9060.
Mission of Libya to the UN: email: <lbyun@undp.org>.
Canada: Libyan People's Bureau, 81 Metcalfe Street, Suite 1000, Ottawa, Ontario, K1P 6K7; tel: 613 230 0919/0683; <www.libya-canada.org>.

EMERGENCIES

The first point of contact for all emergencies should be the security/ tourist policeman and national guide allocated to your tour group. If you're away from the group, then get help from any tourist policeman at a site, hotel reception or other group guide. For a medical emergency, it is better to go direct to the nearest hospital or clinic. There are emergency numbers – Tripoli tel: (021) 444 5581 – but it is unlikely that English will be spoken.

G

GAY AND LESBIAN TRAVELLERS

Even though homosexuality is illegal in Libya, gay and lesbian visitors will encounter few problems as long as they are discreet and cautious about any outward signs of affection towards each other.

GETTING TO LIBYA

By Air *(See also Airports.)* Most visitors will arrive at Tripoli International Airport, but it is also possible to use Benghazi or Sebha airports. Airlines flying direct to Tripoli from European cities include British Airways (operated through its subsidiary British Mediterranean), tel: (021) 335 1278/9; Lufthansa; KLM; Alitalia; Swissair; Austrian; Czech; Balkan; Olympic; Air Malta; Turkish Airlines and Aeroflot. Tunis Air, Egypt Air, Royal Air Maroc and Air Algérie also fly from Europe, and passengers from North America will have to connect with one of these flights. Most flights are not daily, so check websites for information.

Afriqiyah Airways, tel: (021) 444 9734; <www.Afriqiyah.aero> is a new Libyan airline, which has flights to London, Paris, Geneva and Brussels, as well as African connections to Abidjan, Accra, Bamako, Cotonou, Khartoum, Lagos, Lome, N'Djamena, Niamey and Ouagadougou. As Libya expands its own airlines, check the following to see what they have to offer:

Buraq Air, tel: (021) 350 0821 or 351 0016; <www.Buraqair.com> flies internally but also has charter flights to Istanbul.

Libyan Arab Airlines (LAA) tel: (021) 361 6732/9, 333 0060; is the old government airline, which operates internal and international routes.

By Road The popular overland route from Tunisia has been used during and since sanctions. Libyan tour agencies are used to meeting and assisting tourists at the Ras Djejir border crossing, 170km (105 miles) west of Tripoli, for those who land at Djerba and organise a combined Tunisia/Libya itinerary. Officials can now issue visas if the correct paperwork has been prepared *(see Customs and Entry Requirements)*.

The eastern border crossing with Egypt at M'saad (al-Burdi) 140km (90 miles) from Tobruk, is for those with an Egypt/Libya schedule. Border crossings with southern neighbours Sudan, Chad, Niger and Algeria are remote and subject to change.

By Sea Currently there are no regular ferries into the country. However, the relaxation of entry formalities and visas will make it much easier for cruise ships to include coastal archaeological sites in Libya in their Mediterranean itineraries in future.

From Tripoli there are full-day coastal tours to Leptis Magna and Sabratha. Benghazi harbour is shallow and can only handle smaller ships offering tours to Cyrene and Apollonia. The ban on alcohol does not apply to visitors staying on board cruise ships, but the bar has to close while the ship is in Libyan waters, and of course, no alcohol can be brought ashore.

GUIDES AND TOURS
(see also CUSTOMS AND ENTRY REQUIREMENTS)

Unlike most countries, it is still not possible simply to arrive and travel independently around Libya. All tourists (including those on cruises) must be 'invited' by an officially recognised tour agency, which will arrange visas, itineraries, accommodation, transport, permissions and paperwork. They can do this directly with you on a one-off basis (can be expensive), or work with tour operators worldwide to offer one- and two-week group tours on set departure dates.

In Libya, there are hundreds of tour agencies, but few who have the experience or connections to make your trip as hassle-free as possible. Some specialise in French, Italian or German groups. Among those to be recommended are:

Alawy (based in Sebha): tel: (071) 632211; fax: (071) 632244; Tripoli office: tel: (021) 478 1531; fax: (021) 477 7267; email: <alawy@alawytours.com>; <www.alawytours.com>.

Arkno: tel: (021) 444 1452/2010; fax: (021) 333 0530; email: <info@arkno.com>; <www.arkno.com>.

Fezzan: tel: (021) 483 2771; fax: (021) 333 9815; email: <info@fezzantours.com>; <www.fezzantours.com>.

Libtra: tel: (021) 489 6697/6468; fax: (021) 489 6698; email: <info@libtratours.com>; <www.libtratours.com>.

Wings: tel: (021) 333 1855 or 334 1655; fax: (021) 333 0881; email: <info@wingstours.com>; <www.wingstours.com>.

Winzrik: tel: (021) 361 1123/4/5; fax: (021) 361 1126; email: <wts@winzrik.com>; <www.winzrik.com>.

H

HEALTH AND MEDICAL CARE (see also EMERGENCIES)

All public medical facilities in Libya are free, but there is a growing private clinic sector. Most tourists are directed to this private sector, which initially has to be paid for direct and reclaimed from travel insurance. In rural areas there are usually public hospitals with overseas doctors speaking English (many are from Eastern Europe) who will come to attend sick or injured visitors. For minor ailments, local pharmacies are helpful. Drink bottled water and avoid food that is not freshly cooked. Keep out of the sun and take high factor suncream, sunglasses and a hat for protection. Full health insurance is recommended.

Get a doctor…	**Jeeb doktor…**
quickly	**bisoorah**
hospital	**mustashfa**

Vaccinations: Nothing is compulsory, but polio, tetanus, typhoid and hepatitis A are recommended, as is a course of anti-malaria tablets, despite the small risk. Check at <www.mdtravelhealth.com>.

HOLIDAYS

There are two types of official holidays, secular (fixed dates) and religious, which move forward roughly 11 days every year with the Islamic calendar. The fixed holidays are:

2 March	Declaration of the Jamahirya
22 March	Arab League Day

28 March	Departure of British forces
11 June	Departure of American forces
23 July	Nasser's revolution
1 September	Al Fatah revolution anniversary
7 October	Departure of Italian forces

Libya's variable holidays, which change with the Islamic calendar, are as follows:

- **Fatih Muharram**   Islamic New Year
- **Ashura Day**   Remembers the assassination of Hussein
- **Prophet Mohammed's birthday**
- **Eid al-Fitr (The Minor Feast)**   Three-day celebration, end of Ramadan
- **Eid al-Adha (The Grand Feast)**   Commemorates the sacrifice of Abraham

L

LANGUAGE

The official language is Arabic, which must be used for all official purposes. Many Libyans also know some Italian, with English normally understood by people working in hotels and restaurants. All road, shop and other signs, even hotels, are in Arabic.

The only other languages you are likely to encounter are Nafusi (Berber), spoken in the Berber strongholds of Jebel Nafusa, and Tamasheq, spoken by the Touareg in the area around Ghat.

Some useful Arabic words and phrases:

yes/no	**aywa/la**
hello	**salam aleykum**
(response to hello)	**aleykum salam**
hello/welcome	**ahlan wa sahlan**

OK	**bahi**
please	**min fadlak**
thank you	**shukran**
(response to thank you)	**afwan**
How are you?	**Kayf halik?**
I am fine	**al humdillilah**
good morning	**sabah al-kher**
good evening	**mesa al-kher**
What is your name?	**Aish esmak?**
My name is….	**Izmi…**
I do not understand	**Ana mush fahem**
Do you speak English?	**Inta bititkalem inglizi?**
I would like…	**Nebi…**
water	**moyya**
tea	**shay**
coffee	**khawa** (or **Nescafé**)
the bill	**al hessab**
dinner	**asha**
Where is...?	**Waine…?**
hotel	**fonduq**
market	**souq**
museum	**mat haf**
mosque	**jama**
goodbye	**ma'a salama**

M

MAPS

Two maps available in Tripoli are the red *Libya* (published by Cartographia in Hungary) and the slightly more detailed green *Map of the Socialist People's Libyan Arab Jamahiriya* (published by Malt International in Lebanon). The latter has more information, being printed on both sides. Both have close-up details of Tripoli, Benghazi and Jebel Nafusa, and are usually obtainable at Dar Fergiani Publishers on 1 September Street, Tripoli; tel: (021) 444 4873.

Tour agencies generally hand out archaeological site maps to their groups. Maps on the desert regions are almost non-existent.

MEDIA

Newspapers: There is a bi-weekly newspaper in English in Libya called *The Tripoli Post*, produced in offices in Tripoli and published also in Malta. Some English international newspapers are available, but other imported papers and magazines are hard to find, mainly due to the strict censorship rules.

The main Arabic dailies are *Al-Fajir al-Jadid*, *Al-Shams*, *Al-Jamahiriya* and *Az-Zahf al-Akhdar*.

> Have you any English papers? **Hal fee jereeda ingliziya?**

Television: Most hotel rooms will have a television set, but not all have satellite, so you may be limited to the two state-run Libyan TV channels. Each evening Channel 2 has limited-interest news coverage in French and English. Those with satellite reception can usually get BBC World, CNN and other global networks.

Radio: Great Jamahiriya Radio is state-run, and there are a number of local radio stations based in the major cities. Voice of Africa is the state-run external service. Short-wave radios can usually pick up the BBC World Service, Voice of America and a reasonable selection of music from Italian stations.

MONEY

Currency: The unit is the Libyan dinar (LD), which is divided into 1000 dirhams (or 100 piastres). There are banknotes for 20LD,

10LD, 5LD, 1LD, 0.5LD and 0.25LD, with some denominations having three versions in circulation. In 2005, notes starting 1, 2 or 3 before the fraction sign were withdrawn from circulation. Coins are rarely used now, but consist of 500, 250, 100, 50, 20, 10, 5 and 1 dirhams.

Bank and currency exchange: Libya is a cash society, so bring enough foreign currency to exchange into dinars to pay for every expenditure. Currency declaration forms are no longer issued on arrival, and official bank-exchange receipts are not required for departure. The exchange rate is linked directly with the US dollar. Only small amounts of LD currency are allowed to be taken in and out of the country.

I want to change some dollars	**Ureed usareef dollar**

Travellers' cheques: Not all banks accept travellers' cheques, and if they do, the conversion process can be time-consuming, so it's better not to depend on them.

Credit cards: Top-end hotels and shops are slowly accepting plastic, but it is still hit and miss as to which cards and at what rate. Again, do not depend on them.

Cash: It's advisable to bring US dollars as cash to exchange, even though at the airport you can also exchange euros and sterling. The majority of top hotels have money-exchange facilities. Theoretically you can re-exchange any surplus dinars at the airport, but you will need a photocopy of your passport to do this and you will also need to be prepared to accept any rate, regardless of what is advertised. For visitors leaving by road, money-changers at the border will convert excess LD into Tunisian or Egyptian currency.

O

OPENING TIMES

Libya operates a six-day working week. Friday is the official day off for all businesses. Business hours are 7am–2pm Sat–Thur.

Banks: Generally open 8am–1pm Sat–Thur and also (possibly in winter) Sat and Wed afternoons, 3.30–5pm.

Post office and government offices: 7am–2pm Sat–Thur in summer, 8am–3pm in winter.

Shops: Generally 9am–2pm and 5–8pm.

Archaeological sites: Usually 8am–5.30pm daily.

Museums: Monday is the official day off for all the museums, otherwise they tend to follow the site opening times. However, they are notorious for closing for weeks without notice or opening for reduced hours.

Mornings are always the best times to get things done, especially during the month of Ramadan, when the working habits change and businesses often open again after sunset.

P

PHOTOGRAPHY

The best advice is to bring all photographic equipment and film with you, although in case of emergency there are good camera shops in all large towns and cities.

Professional and slide films are not sold, but standard 35mm colour-print film is always available. Do not take photographs of women, anyone in uniform, any official, or government or military buildings. In public areas, indicate that you wish to take a picture and stop if anyone objects.

At each site you will need to buy yourself an entry ticket plus an additional camera ticket (5LD for still cameras, 10LD for video). Museums charge in addition to the sites. If you look too professional with tripod and lights you could be stopped and directed to the Antiquity Department, and asked to pay the 'professional fee' of 1,000LD. Inside poorly lit museums you might need to use flash, but take care when photographing white marble statues and mosaics because of the reflection. Desert trips need special care to keep heat and dust out of equipment and films cool.

Can I have a camera ticket?	**Mumkin akhud tothkarat kamara?**
I want a camera film/battery	**Ureed film kamara/battariya**

Digital photography is still something of an unknown here, so again you need to be self-sufficient. *(For recharging batteries, see Electricity.)*

POLICE

In a group visit, you will always be accompanied by a tourist policeman who acts as a security officer. This ensures that you will not be held up unreasonably at checkpoints. Most of them carry weight when, for example, you arrive at a site to find it locked for whatever reasons.

In the unlikely situation that you manage to get permission to travel around alone, you must ensure that you have the correct paperwork stating that you are travelling correctly without a tourist policeman, otherwise you could be considered to have 'escaped' illegally from your group!

POST OFFICES

There are post offices in all towns and cities (open Sat–Thur 7am–2pm in summer and 8am–3pm in winter, closed Fri), but services are generally poor and erratic, and mail may be subject to censorship. Postcards with stamps can also be bought at some shops and souvenir outlets. Main post offices, especially at Maydan al-Jazayir in Tripoli, also specialise in selling collectors' stamps with whole sheets telling stories of episodes in Libya's history.

Airmail to Europe and North America can take anything upwards of two weeks.

A stamp for	**Tab'a bareed Ingilterra,**
England, please	**min fadlak**
airmail	**bareed jowi**

PUBLIC TRANSPORT

Internal Flights: New airlines are starting to open up internal routes *(see Getting to Libya for telephone numbers)*. Flights are cheap considering the distances involved, and the planes are mostly Boeing or Airbus.

Buraq Air <www.Buraqair.com> flies daily between Tripoli and Benghazi, and another 11 destinations internally. Libyan Arab Airlines (LAA) is the government airline which operates Tripoli–Benghazi, also Tripoli–Sebha and an irregular service Benghazi–Sebha. For large groups it might be worth investigating private hire to fly to Ghadames, Ghat or Tobruk. There can be problems with overbooking, confirmations and cancellations, but the situation is generally improving.

Buses: While they are cheap and reliable, some of the longer services wait for more passengers if too few turn up. As most tourists will usually be on a tight schedule and distances in Libya are great, it would be better to look at using improved internal flights.

Shared taxis: The best way to travel short distances between 10 and 300km (5–200 miles) is to use the highly developed system of shared taxis. Every town has a terminus (larger cities have several) from which shared taxis, usually large Peugeot estates, leave as soon as they are full. As prices are so cheap, especially if time is pressing, you can 'buy' any unsold seats in order to get the trip under way. Over longer distances you can have trouble at checkpoints if you are without a security policeman or the correct paperwork. Shared taxis only run between the main urban centres, so you might find that you are still several kilometres from the ancient site that you wish to visit.

Trains: There has been no train service in Libya since 1965, but there are plans to construct new lines along the Tripolitanian coast and another from Tobruk into Egypt.

R

RELIGION

The state religion is Islam, and approximately 97 percent of the population are Sunni Muslims following the Malikite school, which is conservative but not fundamentalist. Since the 1969 coup there has been a concerted effort to reaffirm Islamic values, culture and lifestyle. Islamic law allows men to have up to four wives, but it is now unusual for a man to have more than one.

Some existing religious buildings, such as the Roman Catholic cathedral in Tripoli, have been converted into mosques. It is forbidden for non-Muslims to enter any mosque, tomb or other Islamic site, but sometimes the guardian of a site will allow you to have a quick look around.

Religious freedom is respected by Muslims, and there are regular Masses in English, Italian, French, Arabic, Polish and Korean at San Francisco Catholic Church in Tripoli's al-Dahra district (in English on Sunday 10am and noon; Mon–Thur 6pm; Fri 10.30am and 4pm). There are no Jews remaining in Libya, but their holy sites are respected, such as the old synagogue in Yefren.

T

TELEPHONES

Codes: The international code for Libya is 218.

Area codes within Libya:	
Tripoli	**21**
Benghazi	**61**
Derna	**81**
Ghadames	**484**
Leptis	**31**
Misrata	**51**
Sabratha	**24**
Sebha	**71**
Sirte	**54**

Mobile telephones: GSM 900 and 1800 networks are in use; providers include Al Madar GSM 900 (Vodafone now has coverage via Vodafone Malta, through the Al Madar network) and Libyana (coverage of Tripoli, Benghazi and Sebha); Thuraya (based in the United Arab Emirates) works by satellite and even gets connections in remote parts of the Fezzan.

Public phone boxes: These are used for national and local calls only.

TIME DIFFERENCES

Libya is one hour ahead of the UK in summer, and two hours ahead in winter. The whole country operates on one time zone, being two hours ahead of GMT (with no Daylight Saving Time in summer). The country is so vast that sunset on the eastern border with Egypt is almost one hour before sunset on the Tunisian border. With this in mind, the chart above opposite gives **summer** time differences.

New York	London	**Tripoli**	Sydney	Auckland
6am	11am	**noon**	8pm	10pm

TIPPING

There is not a great tradition of tipping in Libya, and it has only recently been introduced. For restaurants and cafés you could give the waiter 10 percent and for helpful hotel staff offer 1 or 2LD. Site guides would appropriate 5–10LD at the end of their tour. For drivers, national guides and security/tourist police who are with you for the length of your visit, calculate around 1LD per day from each member of the group. Always agree a fee with a taxi driver and do not add a tip.

TOILETS

Apart from at airports and some of the larger tourist sites, there are no public toilets in Libya. In urban areas ask in a café, restaurant or hotel, and you can even ask at the local mosque. In the countryside, make sure that you are well away from people and houses before disappearing behind a bush, and remember always to carry toilet paper with you, just in case.

toilet	**al-hammam**

TOURIST INFORMATION

Tourism development surveys have been completed by the UN Development Programme on behalf of the Libyan government, but it is left to the private sector to promote and implement their recommendations. So in place of tourist offices, it is the tour agencies who produce any useful tourist information, including hotel particulars, reservations, travel arrangements and site maps. For further details, visit their websites (*see Guides and Tours,* and *Websites and Internet Cafés*).

W

WATER

The safest thing is to avoid tap water in all places. Bottled water from several local sources (including the Great Man-Made River brand) is cheap and available everywhere.

WEBSITES AND INTERNET CAFÉS

There are now many internet cafés with cheap rates all over the country. With the development of tourism in the hands of the private sector, most of the larger tour agencies have their own websites with useful tourist and practical information *(see Guides and Tours)*. Many of the following sites also have useful links:

For information and facts:
• <www.libyaonline.com> has tourism facts on the country
• <www.libyana.org> Libyan culture plus downloadable Libyan music
• <www.hejleh.com/countries/libya.html> a vast number of useful links
• <http://en.marweb.com/libya/> has many North African links
• <http://www.arab.de/arab/Arab_Countries/Libya/> has links to many sites, including the link to the Libya page at the US State Department, <www.state.gov>
• <www.yellowpages.ly> contact information, part of Libyaonline
• <www.Janzour.com> has many good links and information

For news and topical comments:
• <www.afol.com/countries/libya>
• <www.allafrica.com/libya/>
• <www.libya1.com>

The **official internal sites**, for state information, are:
• <www.alfarajaljadeedeng.com> news in English from the daily paper
• <www.jamahiriyanews.com>

• <www.mathaba.net> the official Gaddafi site including the *Green Book* online

Official external sites:
• <www.fco.gov.uk> official advice and information from the UK Foreign Office
• <www.britain-in-libya.com> the British Embassy site in Tripoli has up-to-date-travel information and advice

WOMEN TRAVELLERS

Most women visiting Libya will tell you how safe they generally feel. Accepted by both genders, women visitors are in a great position to be 'honorary men' when dealing with the open public world of Libyan men, but they are also of interest to local women, who are keen to meet them and discuss topics of interest. An invitation by a Libyan woman into a private house should be eagerly accepted. Single women should not wander alone at night in quiet areas such as closed *souqs* and medinas.

Y

YOUTH HOSTELS

One alternative to the shortage of hotels is to use the small but effective network of youth hostels, which are basic but generally clean, with beds in dormitories and shared bathrooms. Details at <www.hihostels.com>. There are hostels in all the main towns and cities and some near the major sites, but information is vague about temporary closures. Some hostels have become centres for (mainly sub-Saharan) immigrant workers, and are effectively men-only. Most hostels are open throughout the year, 7–10.30am and 2pm–midnight, with reception open 2pm–midnight.

Purchase a Hostelling International membership card in your home country before arrival. The HQ of the Libyan YHA is at the central youth hostel in Tripoli, 69 Amr Ben Al-Aas Street, PO Box 10322; tel: (021) 444 5171; fax: (021) 333 0118.

Recommended Hotels

At present most hotels are booked for tourists by agencies as part of an inclusive tour. However, as restrictions are relaxed you should have more options to choose the standard you want, even though an official tour agency may still need to make the booking for you.

At some locations there is little or no choice, and most of the suitable hotels for tourists are included in the following list. However, as the private sector embraces the expansion in tourism, new hotels are continually being planned and built. The only top-class hotels are in the major cities of Tripoli and Benghazi.

As a basic guide, the symbols are for a double room with private facilities and air-conditioning. Always expect to pay cash (US dollars or Libyan dinars) either direct to the hotel or through a local travel agency (ie no credit cards). Generally breakfast is included.

$$$$$	US$250 and above
$$$$	US$125–250
$$$	US$80–125
$$	US$50–80
$	under US$50

TRIPOLI

Al-Kebir (Grand Hotel) $$$ *al-Fatah Street; tel: (021) 444 5940-58, (021) 360 6781-90; fax: (021) 444 5959, (021) 360 6781.* Very central hotel near Green Square with city or sea views, used by government, diplomats and tourists, but now starting to show its age. Pool, sauna, business centre, bookshop and useful money exchanges. Coffee shop and first-floor restaurant overlooking the harbour. 132 rooms.

Al-Mahari $$$$ *al-Shaut Street; tel: (021) 333 4091-6 or 444 9075-9; fax: (021) 444 9094.* Large 15-storey hotel to the east of the city, overlooking the harbour and popular with visiting officials.

Great views from the higher floors. Pool, gym, sauna, souvenir shop and business centre. 24-hour coffee shop and panorama terrace restaurant overlooking the city. 268 rooms and 13 suites.

Bab al-Bahr $$$ *Sharia al-Corniche; tel: (021) 335 0676; fax: (021) 335 0711.* Large 16-floor seashore hotel situated 15 minutes' walk southwest of the Medina. Three restaurants and summer swimming pool. Good service, although the hotel is generally a little past its best. Slightly confusing breakfast layout. 400 rooms and 12 suites.

Corinthia Bab Africa $$$$$ *Souk al-Thulatha al-Gadim; tel: (021) 335 1990; fax: (021) 335 1992; email: <tripoli@corinthia. com>; <www.corinthiahotels.com>.* By far the best hotel in Libya, opened in 2003 in a dramatic location on the Medina seafront. All rooms on the 26 floors have excellent views over the sea or the Medina, with executive rooms on the higher floors. Indoor and outdoor swimming pools, spa, sauna, *hammam*, fitness room, executive club and business centre. Five top-class restaurants featuring Libyan, Moroccan, Italian and Oriental cuisine. 299 rooms including 79 suites.

Safwa $$$ *Baladia Street; tel: (021) 444 3257, (021) 333 4422, (021) 333 4592; fax: (021) 444 9062, (021) 333 2019; email: <safwa24@hotmail.com>; <www.safwahotel.com>.* Also known as the Safaa, this is a pleasant suites-only hotel near the old People's Palace. Mostly for business guests; all spacious rooms have computer, refrigerator and safe. Good restaurant and coffee bar in gardens. 20 suites.

Winzrik $$ *al-Shat Street, Zawet al-Dahmani; tel: (021) 484 62485, (021) 340 3570/8, (021) 340 3946/7; fax: (021) 340 3579.* Small hotel now refurbished and owned by the Winzrik Group, east of the al-Mahari hotel. Souvenir shop and restaurant with daily dish of the day. Good value. 14 rooms.

Yosser $$ *Anter Street, al-Dahra; tel: (021) 444 0775, (021) 334 1352, (021) 333 0911; fax: (021) 334 1321.* Located 200m/yds from the front of the San Francisco Church, this new six-floor hotel is owned by Wings Travel. The restaurant on the top floor has great views over the harbour and city, serving only breakfast. Good value. 30 rooms.

JANZOUR

Janzour Beach Resort $$$ *Tourist village in Janzour town 15km (9 miles) east of Tripoli; tel: (021) 489 0430-5; fax: (021) 489 0521.* Pleasant complex of apartments and chalets right on the beach, with indoor and outdoor pools, restaurants and café, bowling alley, tennis court and dive centre. Very popular, it tends to be fully booked by Libyans through the summer. The town has its own useful website <www.janzour.com>.

BENGHAZI

Al-Fadeel $$ *al-Shat Street, al-Jazira Avenue; tel: (061) 909 9790/5, (061) 909 5300; fax: (061) 909 3642; email: <elfadeel hotel@hotmail.com>.* Newly refurbished hotel in Juliana district beyond the Ouzo Hotel. Situated near the sea with private beach, restaurant and terrace coffee shop. Some rooms with computer and internet access. 65 rooms.

Ouzo $$$$ *al-Buhira Street; tel: (061) 909 5160-6; fax: (061) 909 2110; email: <info@uzuhotel.com>; <www.uzuhotel.com>.* Six-floor hotel on the western shore of 23 July Lake with business centre, internet café, shops and money exchange. Coffee shop and restaurant on ground floor, with extensive buffet breakfast. Pleasant 20-minute walk across road bridge into old city. 238 rooms and 24 suites.

Tibesti $$$$ *Jamal Abdul Nasser Street; tel: (061) 909 8029/31, (061) 909 0016/7; fax: (061) 909 7160; <www.tibestyhotel.com>.* Luxury hotel ideally situated downtown on eastern edge of 23 July Lake. Swimming pool, health club, business centre, four restaurants and two coffee shops, one of which is on the 15th floor with fabulous views over the lake. Offices of Lufthansa, Tunis Air and Egypt Air. 220 rooms and 22 luxury suites.

YEFREN

Yefren Tourism $$ *In the Old Town; tel: (0421) 60278; fax: (021) 483 0117; <www.yefrenhotel.com>*. Recently refurbished Italian hotel that was popular during colonial times. Modern rooms and facilities with restaurant and lovely panorama terrace looking over the Nafusa Mountains.

GHADAMES

Al-Waha $$$ *1km (½ mile) from town centre on road to Tripoli; tel: (0484) 62569; fax: (0484) 62568*. Pleasantly situated bungalows around courtyard. Restaurant and camp ground. The best available yet, used by large groups, but a 20-minute walk to town. 40 rooms.

Kafila $$ *In New Town past the large mosque; tel: (0484) 62991; fax: (0484) 62176; email: <kafilahotel69@hotmail.com>*. Much used by groups, but getting a little threadbare. Restaurant and coffee shop. 22 rooms.

Winzrik Motel $$ *Beside the Old City; tel/fax: (0484) 62485*. Motel offering basic comfortable accommodation and its own restaurant. Part of the Winzrik group. 16 rooms.

ZLITEN

Zliten $$ *On main road through town; tel: (0521) 620121-7; fax: (0521) 620120; email: <zlitenhotel@lttnet.net>*. Good comfortable rooms, useful for Leptis Magna. Restaurant and coffee shop, or 10-minute walk into centre for local restaurants. 64 rooms and 4 suites.

BENI WALID

Zaitouna $ *In town centre; tel: (0322) 221040-4; fax: (0322) 61011*. Good new hotel ideally placed for Ghirza region. Restaurant and coffee shop with views from terrace over Wadi Merdun. 36 rooms.

MISRATA

Ghoz-alteek $$$ *al-Dairy al-Oual Street, near the Burj Ghoz-alteek monument; tel: (051) 614614, 613333; fax: (051) 610500.* This large hotel, with amenities including three restaurants and pool, is mainly used by groups when visiting Leptis Magna. 132 rooms, 16 suites and 17 bungalows.

GHARYAN

Rabta $$ *In town centre; tel: (041) 631970-4; fax: (041) 631972.* A centrally located, older-style block mainly used by visiting officials. Amenities include a passable restaurant and coffee bar. 68 rooms.

SEBHA

Al-Jebel $$ *On top of hill 6km (4 miles) east of town; tel: (071) 629407-9; fax: (071) 629481.* Sebha is the best hotel in the Fezzan, but because of that it can sometimes be taken over by diplomats and officials. Amenities include a restaurant and café. Great views too. 24 rooms and 1 suite.

SIRTE

Al-Mahari $$ *5km (3 miles) west of city centre; tel: (054) 60100-4; fax: (054) 61310.* A large hotel, located in its own grounds 500m (546 yds) from the beach. It is quiet and well appointed, with a good restaurant and coffee shop. A useful midway stop between Tripoli and Benghazi. 50 rooms.

SUSA

Al-Manara $$ *Seafront; tel: (0851) 63030-4; fax: (0851) 63035; email: <info@manarahotel.com>; <www.manarahotel.com>.* A new hotel excellently situated at the gates of Apollonia site. All rooms have some kind of sea view. There's a good restaurant and coffee shop with fabulous views from Susa café on seventh floor. 66 rooms and 24 suites.

Recommended Restaurants

There are some good restaurants in the main cities, but there may not be much choice in smaller towns apart from local chicken or fast-food places. As most Libyans do not tend to eat out, the majority in this list will be frequented by tourists or foreign businessmen. Apart from specialising in fish, there is often little difference in most menus, which usually have a choice of local, North African and Italian dishes. Fish can sometimes become quite expensive if priced by weight. Some of the larger hotel restaurants offer international cuisine.

Telephone numbers are included as most restaurants are relatively small, and can be full with one tour group. It is well worth booking ahead or at least finding out when they might be busy, unless you are happy to take pot luck with the local places. Some are open all day, others close between lunch and dinner, most close Friday lunchtime. Do not leave it too late as most restaurants shut around 10pm. Most do not have signs in English, so practise your Arabic or ask near by.

As a guide, expect to pay the following for a three-course meal:

$$$$	over US$40
$$$	US$25–40
$$	US$10–25
$	under US$10

TRIPOLI

Al-Burei $ *38, Trigh al-Helga alley in the Medina; tel: (021) 444 3556.* Lunch-only place with great choice of local dishes. Small, crowded, lively and good fun. It's tricky to find – for directions, *see page 32.*

Al-Saraya $$ *Green Square, opposite the Red Castle; tel: (021) 333 4433/4.* New two-storey circular building, ideally placed overlooking Green Square. Café downstairs and in gardens, international restaurant upstairs with daily specials such as Lebanese *Kharouf mehche* lamb and *Siyadieh* fish.

Al-Sheraa $$ *In lively western suburb of Gargaresh; tel: (021) 477 5123; fax: (021) 478 0228.* This large establishment is ideal for bigger groups or – since it's located in a suburb of Tripoli – for those wanting to get away from the city centre.

Athar $$$ *Beside the Arch of Marcus Aurelius, Old City; tel: (021) 444 7001.* Athar offers a good range of dishes, including couscous and *tajine,* and is popular with groups at both lunch and dinner. It is set in an ideal location, and is particularly lovely in summer, when diners can sit at the terraces overlooking the arch, which is illuminated at night. It's the most visible of the three restaurants run by the Shames brothers; the others are Ghazala and al-Sheraa *(see opposite and above).*

Az-Zareeq $$ *Seafront beyond al-Kebir (Grand) Hotel; tel: (021) 361 1123-5; fax: (021) 361 1126; <www.winzrik.com>.* A complex of different restaurants including Lebanese café, Indian restaurant and à la carte, as well as large hall for wedding parties etc. Part of the Winzrik Group, who also recently converted an old house, ad-Dar in the Medina opposite the Old British Consulate, into dining rooms.

Corinthia Bab Africa $$$$ *Souk al-Thulatha al-Gadim; tel: (021) 335 1990; fax: (021) 335 1992.* The Corinthia Bab Africa offers the opportunity to sample high-quality food even if you are not staying at the top-class hotel. The Venezia and Oriental restaurants are à la carte, as is the Moroccan restaurant Fes (on the 26th floor), which offers grand views over the city. There is a good-value international buffet at La Vallete for both lunch and dinner, and the Tripoli café for light snacks.

Diafa Fish $$ *Baladia Street, behind the al-Kebir (Grand) Hotel; tel: (021) 444 5757; mobile: 091 370 7930.* As the name suggests, a small speciality fish restaurant, located only a stone's throw from Green Square.

Galaxy $$ *135, 1 September Street, opposite Islamic Arts and Crafts School; tel: (021) 444 8764; mobile: 091 213 4412.* Small, lively two-floor place, offering speciality *jarra* meat cooked in a pot if ordered at least three hours before dining.

Gambare $$$ *Baladia Street, behind the al-Kebir (Grand) Hotel; tel: (021) 334 1287, mobile: 091 212 3052.* Close to Green Square, this is a small, intimate speciality fish restaurant. Meat dishes are also served.

Ghazala $$ *10-minute walk from Green Square in al-Dahra district; tel: (021) 444 7000.* Run by Fakher Hussein Shames, this is a friendly, award-winning fish restaurant with live music. The good-value set menu, salad buffet and à la carte menu are popular with groups.

Mourjan $$ *Meydan al-Jazayir, opposite main post office; tel: (021) 333 6307; mobile: 092 507 6236, 092 310 9318.* Mourjan does fish as a speciality and offers a good-value set menu. It's especially popular with businessmen in the area.

Salim $$ *Under arches on Green Square, end of 1 September Street; tel: (021) 333 3024; mobile: 091 210 0958.* Established in 1984, this place has a lively café with fast food below and a good restaurant with a large menu and views across to the Medina gate above.

BENGHAZI

Al-Arabi $$ *Sports City near Ouzo Hotel; tel: (061) 909 4468.* One of several restaurants at southern end of the lake, identified by a large blue anchor on wall outside. Interesting decor including some floor-sitting areas, with fine seafood and good-value set menu. Also offers *jarra* speciality with six hours' notice. Ask your taxi driver for al-Butrique, which is the fast-food café downstairs.

Al-Kabeer $$ *Jamal Abdul Nasser Street opposite Mumtaz Hotel; tel: (061) 908 1692; mobile: 092 511 1545.* Popular and lively Turkish restaurant with good choice of dishes. In busy location on edge of old city, run by Jehad Yousef Alci and family.

Gharnata $$ *Jamal Abdul Nasser Street, opposite Tibesti Hotel; tel: (061) 909 0107; mobile: 092 512 9164.* Turkish restaurant with good-value set menu and vegetarian options.

Libika $$$ *Sports City near Ouzo Hotel; mobile: 092 510 8291.* Situated at the far end of several restaurants on southern end of the lake, decorated like a fisherman's shack and not surprisingly specialising in fish.

Matam Rabir $ *At traffic lights on 23 July Street, at corner of lake; tel: (061) 909 5656.* Quality fast-food joint situated behind al-Kabeer restaurant, specialising in fresh oven-baked pizza and *shawarma*. Fast and friendly service.

Tibesti $$$ *Jamal Abdul Nasser Street; tel: (061) 909 8029/31, (061) 909 0016/7; fax: (061) 909 7160.* For the best quality in the city, head to this hotel's Shahat restaurant for Italian cuisine overlooking the lake from the 13th floor (evenings only). Otherwise there is Middle Eastern at the Balad al-Toyoub on the third floor. For light meals try the 15th-floor al-Loaloah coffee shop with superb views.

DERNA

Salsabil $$ *On seafront of Old Town; tel: (081) 624863.* Ideally located beside the main Tobruk road for meals or snacks.

GHADAMES

Dan Magrumah $$ *Near the western entrance to Old City* Four-course local meal (couscous, camel etc) in a restored traditional house in the Old City is quite an experience. Should be booked at least the day before through any of the hotels or guides, such as Ahmed Heba, tel: (0484) 62700.

Jewel of the Sahara $ *Beside entrance to Old City; tel: (0484) 62015.* Good-value, family-run place serving simple food in a pleasant atmosphere.

INDEX